HMS
TRINCOMALEE

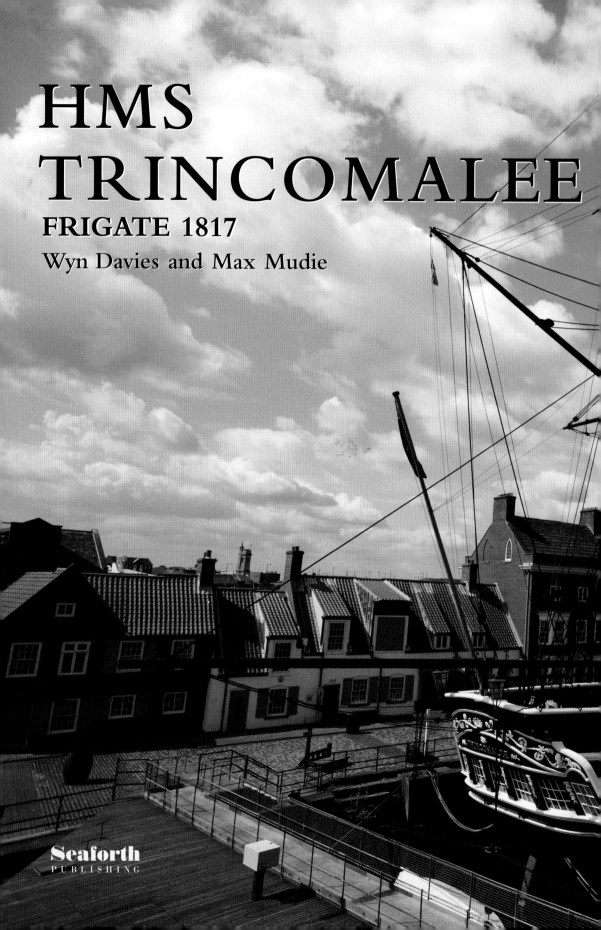

HMS TRINCOMALEE

FRIGATE 1817

Wyn Davies and Max Mudie

Seaforth
PUBLISHING

First published in Great Britain in 2015 by
Seaforth Publishing,
Pen & Sword Books Ltd,
47 Church Street,
Barnsley S70 2AS

www.seaforthpublishing.com

British Library Cataloguing in Publication Data

A catalogue record for this book is available from the
British Library

ISBN 978 1 84832 221 9

Art Direction and Design by Stephen Dent
Deck layouts by Tony Garrett
Printed by Printworks Global Ltd, London & Hong Kong

CONTENTS

Half Title: *Trincomalee's* quarter galleries and a view of the starboard side which shows the main armament of an eighteenth-century frigate.

Title Pages: The historic quay and dock, Hartlepool, where *Trincomalee* lies afloat in all weathers. The masts and yards rise high above the surrounding buildings and in a strong southwesterly she heels in the gusts giving visitors just a small taste of the movement of a ship upon the ocean.

Above left: A general view of the gun deck showing the classic barley sugar twist on the pillars, a feature that was the trademark of the Bombay builders.

Following pages: The view from across the harbour, showing *Trincomalee* behind the lock gates.

FOREWORD

BUILT IN BOMBAY IN 1817, HMS *TRINCOMALEE* is the oldest British warship afloat.

Britain was suffering a shortage of shipbuilding-quality oak early in the nineteenth century after the end of the Napoleonic Wars and, despite being victorious, the British fleet needed refurbishing and rebuilding. Accordingly, the Admiralty placed a contract for a 46-gun, fifth rate, *Leda* Class frigate, *Trincomalee,* to be constructed of Malabar teak. She was built by the famous Master Shipbuilder of the Bombay Dockyard, Jamsetjee Bomanjee Wadia, to the contract which was placed through The Honourable East India Company. *Trincomalee* is unique in being the last remaining fully commissioned frigate of that age.

HMS *Trincomalee* has truly had a long life. The Napoleonic wars were over by the time she arrived in England in 1819 and the world was a much more peaceful place, so she was de-masted, covered over and placed 'in ordinary'. Her active service as a Royal Navy fighting frigate began with her first commission from 1847 – 1850 under the command of Captain Richard Laird Warren on the North American and West Indies Station. Her second commission, from 1852 – 1857, under the command of Captain Wallace Houstoun was on the Pacific Station. Her work during these two commissions included anti-slavery patrols, charting, oceanography, hydrographic survey work and promoting British trade interests overseas.

On her return to Britain, and with the emerging preference for steam ships, she was rapidly becoming outdated. She spent time as a Royal Naval Reserve drill ship, including a fifteen-year spell in Hartlepool, while she spent much of the twentieth century in private hands, as a youth training ship at various ports on the south coast. During this time her name was changed to TS *Foudroyant*.

By 1986, *Foudroyant* was in a poor condition and the nautical training offered was becoming increasingly difficult for schools and young people to use to advantage. The ship was then owned by The Foudroyant Trust, which faced a difficult decision. In these circumstances, the Trustees, under the Chairmanship of Captain David Smith RN, took the momentous decision to cease training.

The Trustees returned the ship to Hartlepool in 1987 and set about raising money to restore her to her second commission configuration of 1852, a process that took nearly eleven years, cost over £10.5m and is considered one of the finest composite restorations in the world. During this process the ship reverted to her original name: HMS *Trincomalee*.

Today, HMS *Trincomalee* is the oldest warship afloat in Europe and the second oldest afloat in the world. Even after covering hundreds of thousands of miles, between the Antarctic and the Artic, the hull contains over sixty per cent of the timber used when she was built nearly two hundred years ago.

Despite the massive restoration she has undergone, her survival depends on a continuing programme of costly maintenance.

You can play your part in helping to preserve this magnificent ship by visiting her in Hartlepool where she's berthed afloat at Jackson Dock, close to the town centre. HMS *Trincomalee* is open all year round and is easy to find – her three towering masts dominate the skyline in this part of town. Please bring your family and friends, all welcome!

David McKnight
General Manager
HMS Trincomalee Trust
www.hms-trincomalee.co.uk

The 38-gun frigate HMS *Pomone*, the second ship of the first batch of *Leda* class frigates ordered in 1802 and built alongside the *Shannon* on the north bank of the Medway at Finsbury, across the river from Rochester. Commissioned in 1806, a successful ship under her second commander, Sir Robert Barrie, she took many prizes in a brief career which ended off the Needles on her way home in 1811. From a colour lithograph by T G Dutton after a painting by G F St John. (© *National Maritime Museum, Greenwich, London, PAH0764*)

1 | HMS TRINCOMALEE

THOSE WITH LONGISH MEMORIES MAY RECALL that Portsmouth was until relatively recently home to more than one Napoleonic era sailing ship. HMS *Victory* is well known, but how many now remember *Implacable* and *Foudroyant*? Now only *Victory* remains, the other two having left in markedly different circumstances. The scuttling in December 1949 of the former (the ex-French *Duguay-Trouin*, a vessel that had also fought at Trafalgar) became the cause célèbre that led to the founding of the World Ship Trust with its motto, 'Never Again', dedicated to the recognition of, and support for, historic vessels. The third ship, *Foudroyant*, however, is still afloat under her original name, HMS *Trincomalee*, and can be found, beautifully restored, in Hartlepool.

Although apparently typical of a frigate of the period, *Trincomalee* has an interesting history and at least one unique feature. She is the only survivor of the warships built for the Royal Navy in Bombay by the East India Company under the Master Builder, Jamsetjee Bomanjee Wadia. As a result of her origins she was constructed of Malabar teak, rather than oak, a fact at least partially responsible for her survival over the years. Teak is perhaps the perfect timber for shipbuilding, its natural oils protecting, rather than attacking, iron fastenings and preserving against rot. So good was it that demand soon outstripped supply, even in a country as vast as India, leading to the British Raj introducing one of the first forestry management schemes, still used in parts of the sub-continent today.

Nelson's quote, 'Was I to die this moment "want of frigates" would be found stamped on my heart', is well known, but it serves to illustrate the importance of the type to the fleet. Being swifter than the ships of the line they were used as the eyes and the ears of the fleet, and also as long distance cruisers, showing the flag, protecting or harassing commercial traffic as the case may be.

The French are often given the credit for developing the type, ones that fitted the French approach of a fast raider, harrying our trade routes, and indeed the French designs were often praised as technically superior by their Royal Navy opponents. However, more careful research suggests that there are some flaws in this deduction, as we shall see. However, it is true that the lines of the *Trincomalee* and her sisters of the *Leda* Class were taken from a French frigate, the *Hébé*.

HMS *Trincomalee* was built in Bombay in 1816–1817, but was laid up in ordinary on arrival in England. She was not commissioned until 1847 when she was re-armed as a corvette. Her only two commis-

HMS *Shannon* engaging the USS *Chesapeake* off Boston, a victorious engagement which restored the Royal Navy's prestige and morale, having lost heavily in engagements with the large American frigates on all previous occasions. Frigates were intended to fight in small numbers or singly. (© *National Maritime Museum, Greenwich, London, BHC0601*)

sions ended in 1857 and in 1860 she became a training or drill ship, sometime in Sunderland, but for a long period in Hartlepool. Subsequently she was sold for breaking up in 1897, but purchased by Geoffrey Wheatley Cobb to replace his previous training ship HMS *Foudroyant*. It was at this time she was renamed *Foudroyant* and was to be moored variously in Falmouth, Milford Haven and finally Portsmouth where our story began.

FRIGATES

Whilst many will have understood the frigate as the glamour ship of the fleet from the writings of such authors as Captain Marryat and Patrick O'Brian, possibly fewer will know just how important these vessels were to the fleet. Nelson's famous quote reveals in part just how much they were needed to keep the fleet informed, but away from the fleet they were the Royal Navy's preferred vessel for convoy escort, commerce raiding, blockade duties and much more.

It is perhaps ironic that the origins of the type are allegedly French whilst their most triumphant users were to be the fledgling US Navy. More recent research suggests that the concept was probably the result of what is now understood as parallel development with the earliest 'large frigate', the *Illurium* appearing in Sweden in 1716. Large frigates have come to be defined as those carrying guns of 18-pounder or larger and were a natural development of the smaller 9- and 12-pounder frigates and so called demi battery ships or old style 6th rates in the Royal Navy. A study of the literature reveals a number of such influences which include the French *guerre de course*, a policy of attacking an enemy's commerce when unable to match its battle fleet, as well as the usual constraints of time and money.

In parallel with this French emphasis on commerce raiding there was also a marked interest in the scientific development of naval architecture in that country which led to claims that French ships were better designed than British. David Brown has suggested that there was an element of salesmanship in this – a captured prize would be worth more if her captor exaggerated the vessel's capabilities. Be that as it may, many successful British ships were built to the lines of captured French vessels including one of the most numerous classes of frigate, the *Leda* class, of which *Trincomalee* is one of two surviving examples. The *Leda* class were based on the lines of the *Hébé*, a design by Jacques-Noël Sané in 1781. So successful was this

design that large numbers were being built well into the nineteenth century, forty-seven being built for the Royal Navy between 1800 and 1830. It is of passing interest to note that Sané's superior, Jean-Charles de Borda, thought that the scientific theories developed in France at the time to be 'useless and even dangerous', so we may suppose that the design for *Hébé* was based on practical extrapolation rather than any new theory!

There is one other survivor of this class in the UK: HMS *Unicorn* resides in Dundee, still in ordinary as she has been since build. *Unicorn* was one of the last group to be built and features many of Sir Robert Seppings' innovations in her structure, giving her a quite different appearance to *Trincomalee* above the waterline.

Unicorn was one of the last, fifth group of *Leda* class frigates to be ordered by the Royal Navy up to 1824. As a result her construction is very different to

A frigate assembling her convoy off the Isle of Wight, possibly the 12-pounder HMS *Triton*. Convoy and escort duty were important roles for frigates. Here she is lying-to with her main topsail backed. (© *National Maritime Museum, Greenwich, London, PAH9534*)

that of *Trincomalee* incorporating as it does the improvements wrought by Seppings in his drive to reduce the amount of compass and large timber needed for warship construction. Compass timber was the naturally curved timber used for frames and the like. Whilst Sepping's innovations, particularly the diag- onal bracing or riders, had the result of producing a stiffer hull they were mainly aimed at reducing the cost of a warship by reducing the demand for timbers which were by this time becoming difficult to source.

Visually two of these improvements can be seen in the rounded stern and full bow of *Unicorn*, removing at last the major weakness of a wooden warship, their vulnerability to raking fire, i.e. fire through the ends sweeping the gun decks from end to end. Other inno- vations that differentiate *Unicorn* from *Trincomalee* include iron knees and diagonal riders.

Like *Trincomalee, Unicorn* was too late to see service in the Napoleonic wars and was laid up in ordinary. Unlike *Trincomalee*, she remained, and still remains, in ordinary. However, like *Trincomalee* she was used as a Royal Naval Reserve drill ship and was moved to Dundee in 1873, where she has remained ever since.

So were French ships really better? Ferreiro covers many scientific advances made by the French, but also demonstrates that some were dead ends whilst others

HMS *Unicorn*

HMS *Unicorn* was built as a 46-gun frigate for the Royal Navy in the Royal Dockyard at Chatham in 1824, to the designs of Sir Robert Seppings, the Surveyor of the Navy, 1813-1832, at a time when the shortage of timber and the growing availability of iron was dramatically affecting the way ships were built. Seppings, who can be thought of as the Royal Navy's Brunel, introduced engineering concepts to warship building. His new methods of construction greatly strengthened

wooden ships, and he took full advantage of the availability, strength and compactness of iron. *Unicorn* represents the last great flourish of wooden shipbuilding and illustrates aspects of the iron steamships that were to follow.

Left: The bow of HMS *Unicorn* showing the massive hull timbers now carried up and around the bow at gun deck level, greatly improving the protection of the gun crews from raking fire.
Above: A similar change of design at the stern of *Unicorn* with the frames and planking now taken up to the bulwarks. *(Photos courtesy the Unicorn Preservation Society)*

were never properly applied. It took several years before all the various threads were drawn together to make what we understand today as naval architectural theory, so it is likely that little, if any, science can be attributed to this claim. It is also generally understood that French ships were somewhat lighter built than British and were thus invariably shorter lived, *pace Duguay-Trouin*. So whilst the hull shapes may have been better, sufficiently so for many of them to be copied, it does not automatically follow that their construction or materials were also better. It probably came down to the skills of individual constructors and captains as much in France as in Britain.

It might be useful for the reader to define what was actually meant by the term frigate in the Royal Navy. A frigate was ship rigged, that is with square sails on three masts, and with a limited armament of 18-pounders or above for large frigates; those with smaller calibre cannon grouped simply as frigates. This armament was to be on a single gun deck arranged above a second complete deck, with the normal addition of guns on the quarter deck and fo'c'sle. This arrangement had the advantage that the guns could be worked in a rougher sea than many two- or three-deckers whose main gun deck was much nearer the waterline and sometimes unusable in rough seas. It

A slightly crude model of a *Leda* class frigate, possibly *Pomone*. The model is unusually rigged with topmasts lowered and no yards or topgallant masts, apparently to demonstrate boat handling procedures. *(© National Maritime Museum, Greenwich, London, SLR0652)*

also allowed a somewhat roomier accommodation for her crew, who did not have to fit themselves around the guns as on ships like the *Victory* for example.

Overall this arrangement resulted in a very 'handy' ship, more manoeuvrable than her bigger cousins and, with her relatively large internal volume, more suited to distant cruising. One that would attract the more adventurous officers, but also one that would serve as an essential step in learning to command a warship for any junior officer.

And the ultimate frigate design? Several would probably point to the USS *Constitution*, built along British lines but with some structural advances that anticipated Seppings by several years. Perhaps the ultimate is HMS *Warrior* which, although leading a revolution in design in so many other ways, is in actual fact just a very large frigate in form.

A sketch of HMS *Shannon*, drawn by Admiral Richard King, who served on her when a midshipman. She is ship rigged and is carrying a very full set of sails, incluuding royals and skysails set above her topgallants, rather in the American tradition. *(From Brighton, Revd J G,* Admiral Sir P B V Broke, Bart, etc: A Memoir, *London 1866)*

2 | WOODEN SHIPBUILDING

IN THE LONG HISTORY OF SEAFARING, WOOD was largely the material of choice, displacing reeds at one end of the time line, before being almost totally displaced by iron and steel in the nineteenth century, ignoring the various composites that are now to be found in some specialised areas. During this vast sprawl of time the actual techniques for building changed but slowly and, as international contacts increased, so regional differences started to disappear, at least in the larger vessels, resulting in warships looking very similar across the globe by the start of the Napoleonic Wars.

Wood does however have its limitations and the size of individual ships grew only slowly such that the largest Spanish galleon would not have been totally overawed by the last wooden warships. Simplistically

put, at its peak wooden shipbuilding generally produced a hull based on a very strong keel, supporting ribs or frames of varying size, depending on the purpose of the vessel, all of which would be covered in planks laid fore and aft. The seams of these planks were then made watertight by some means, usually by caulking with hemp or oakum hammered into the seam and then coated with pitch. The planking was applied both to the ship's sides and to the main decks, the whole resulting in a sound structure capable of carrying large loads whilst negotiating an often lively sea.

The problem with increasing the size of the ship is that the stiffness of this structure, what we would call today the hull girder, is reduced. Stretch it too far and it becomes too flexible. Too much flexing and the planks will work and the caulked seams between will cease to be watertight, a failing observed in the Royal Navy's largest wooden frigates, *Mersey* and *Orlando*, generally agreed to be expensive demonstrations of

A beautifully painted view of the Honourable East India Company docks in Bombay, by Francis Swain Ward. The sterns of the two ships that can be seen in the inner and outer docks indicate that this is somewhat earlier than our period, but well represents the yard as it was when *Trincomalee* was built in the inner dock. *(Courtesy the Martyn Gregory Gallery, London)*

pushing the boundaries too far. The same effect could of course occur by neglecting to maintain the caulking.

Small advances in fastening and jointing techniques, and improved tools, all contributed to what was only a gradual increase in length until the introduction of diagonal bracing and iron fastenings in the early nineteenth century added to the hull's stiffness and allowed a further moderate increase in size. This advance is often attributed to Sir Robert Seppings, master shipwright at Chatham in 1811, but recent research suggests that the diagonal braces to be found in the USS *Constitution* were there from its inception in 1795, several years before Seppings assumed office. It is not known if Seppings was aware of the American designs, but there had been much discussion on the subject of bracing the hull culminating in Seppings' papers of 1814 and 1815. Even this increase in hull stiffness was not sufficient for everyone's needs with Brunel, for example, resorting to bolting every frame to its neighbour down the whole length of the SS *Great Western* to achieve the stiffness he thought necessary for a steam engine, paddlewheel combination. Brunel's next venture, of course, would bring the advent of a new material, iron, which would eventually completely supersede wood for the major navies and merchant fleets.

Seppings' main drive was to reduce the demand for timber, as consumption was exceeding supply. As a result he also introduced the use of iron for knees and his diagonal riders, and redesigned the construction of the frames so fewer grown bends were needed.

With the exception of the introduction of laminated timber this remains the situation for wooden shipbuilding today and the tools used in a modern yard would not seem too different to the Georgian shipwright.

WOOD CONSUMPTION

It will be apparent that a wooden ship of any size consumes a fair number of mature trees. In fact, a warship hull can consume between 2,000 loads for a battleship and 350 loads for a typical frigate, where a standard load is defined as 50 cubic feet. For English oak this would be almost exactly one imperial ton for seasoned timber. This level of demand had quite an early impact on the two main royal sources of supply, the Forest of Dean and the New Forest. Quoting from an on-line History of the New Forest we find, for example, the following report.

> 1707: survey of the Forest by the Navy was undertaken. There were 12,476 trees fit for ship-building (a century earlier in 1608 it was 123,927). This decline was interpreted as a shortage of timber but was probably indicative of

poor administration rather than a true shortage. Naval ships required many mature oaks during construction – in 1781, 2,000 oaks were required for the building of the 64-gun *Agamemnon* at Bucklers Hard in the Forest. *Agamemnon* was considered to be a small ship.

The same source notes that 1862 was the last year in which any quantity of timber was supplied to the Navy, although it also states that oaks planted as a result of the 1808 Enclosure Act were used to build minesweepers during the Second World War.

Two points should be understood when considering the foregoing; it is only the hull that has been dealt with so far and that the load as delivered only contained the usable parts of the tree. A further 45 tons of various timbers would be used in the masting and rigging of a typical frigate.

There are many references to the quantities of oak cut from these two main forests, but it is also clear that they were unable to supply more than a portion of the Navy's needs. Crimmin quotes the annual consumption for 1801 as 36,000 loads rising to 74,000 by 1812. Of this the royal forests could only supply about 4,000 loads. As a result much effort was expended in obtaining good timber overseas, from places as diverse as Southern Russia, Austria and the Ottoman Empire. Other sources were mast timbers from the Baltic and Scandinavia, mast and hull timbers from North America, mahogany from Africa and teak from India and Burma.

WADIA'S SHIPYARD AND BOMBAY

The alternative to shipping timber back to England was to build the ships close to the source of the wood. Many merchant ships were built along the shores of North America, for example, with little more than a saw pit and a set of launching ways. This apparently casual approach was fine if unseasoned timber was used, but somewhat more extensive facilities were needed for the seasoning of timbers for warship building. At this point the Honourable East India Company comes into the story. From their bases in the Indian sub-continent their ships covered an extensive network of trading routes around the Far East. To service this network they had established a shipbuilding industry in Bombay under the oversight of local master-builders, and where teak was the native timber used.

The first military establishment to be set up in India by the British, the Naval Dockyard, Bombay (now Mumbai), has a history spanning over two-and-half centuries. It began with the British shifting their operations from Surat to Bombay in 1686 after they acquired it from the Portuguese and there they gradually developed shipbuilding and repair facilities. In addition to a mud basin set up in 1693-94, covered marine store houses, carpenter's shed, smithy shop, offices and quarters were progressively set up. With this, the yard became a complete facility, the 'Marine Yard' of 1735.

The yard's facilities were developed to keep pace with the shipbuilding requirements which included construction of dry docks, namely Bombay dry dock in 1750-1765 (said to be the first dry dock built in Asia) followed by Duncan Dry Dock in 1808-10, a breakwater in 1830, four slipways, Torpedo Dry Dock in 1892-93 and the Wet Basin in 1889, along with a support infrastructure. Most of these facilities are still in use. From building smaller ships, the yard graduated to building bigger ones, the largest ship built was the 2,591tonne HMS *Madras* (renamed HMS *Meanee*). As many as 275 ships were built during the period 1761-1860.

The history of shipbuilding and Bombay Dockyard is synonymous with the history of the Wadia Master Builder, Jamsetjee Bomanjee Wadia, responsible for *Trincomalee*, plus some fourteen other Royal Navy vessels. In all nine Master Builders and fifteen Assistant Builders of the Wadia family rendered distinguished service during the period 1735-1884.

In fact the Royal Navy had considered starting their own yard in India, but common sense obviously prevailed and the EIC yard was contracted to supply several warships, including four 84-gun ships and at least six 74-gun ships, in addition to many smaller vessels, amongst which were *Trincomalee* and her sister *Amphitrite*.

TEAK

For shipbuilding purposes teak has few if any disadvantages; as noted in the introduction its natural oils protect rather than attack iron fastenings and protect the wood itself against rot, giving it a natural long life expectancy. It was the obvious choice of shipbuilding timber for a Bombay shipyard and such was the demand that the local forests soon became exhausted of decent sized trees.

The most recent procurement of large quantities of teak for marine use from Burma (now Myanmar) was for the re-decking of HMS *Warrior*. Whilst confirming that this timber met modern standards of ethical sourcing it was pointed out by the supplier that Myanmar still used the forestry management system put in place by the British Raj.

A certain Wilhelm Schlich (later Sir William Schlich) entered the British Imperial Indian Forest Service in 1866, becoming Conservator of Forests in 1871, and Inspector-General of Forests in 1883. He developed forest management and education programmes and

The Master Builder of Bombay, Jamsetjee Bomanjee, of the Wadia dynasty. The drawing in his right hand is the stern of HMS *Minden*, a 74-gun ship launched in 1810, one of a number that Bombay built alongside the frigates such as *Trincomalee*. (© *National Maritime Museum, Greenwich, London, BHC2803*)

spent a total of nineteen years in India, helping to establish the journal *Indian Forester* in 1874 and the forestry school at Dehradun in 1877. During his time as Conservator he established the forestry management scheme which is still followed to this day, perhaps one of the first, if not the very first, attempts at environmentalism. His manual for foresters is still available, having been reprinted several times, and is listed in the bibliography here.

Currently teak is used extensively for the decking of yachts and cruise liners where it is applied as a decorative finish rather than for strength. To satisfy this demand plantations of teak have been established in a variety of places. India now rarely exports teak as it consumes most of its production at home. Plantation teak is available from many dry tropical countries from Central and South America to the East Indies and is generally understood to be as good as natural teak, despite myths to the contrary.

3 | TRINCOMALEE'S SERVICE LIFE

TRINCOMALEE WAS FLOATED OUT OF HER
building dock in Bombay on 12 October 1817, inciden-
tally possibly pre-empting this now universal technique
by many years. She was moved to her namesake port
in Ceylon (modern Sri Lanka) initially to be laid up, but
then masted and rigged. She finally set sail for home
on 27 October 1818 under the command of Philip
Henry Bridges, in company with HMS *Fowey*. After a
slow passage home, the Napoleonic Wars being finally
over, she was placed in ordinary and left in what today
would be described as care and maintenance until
further need.

Fortunately the voyage home is well covered in the
diary of Eliza Bunt which, whilst simply written, gives
an interesting insight to the voyage conditions. Eliza
was the widow of John Bunt who, having been
appointed boatswain of Trincomalee dockyard in
1816, had succumbed to fever in 1818. As he was a
dockyard officer the Navy Board had a responsibility to
return Eliza and her two children to England and this
they duly did on board HMS *Trincomalee*. The first leg
of the voyage to Mauritius took them a month, during
which time Eliza records the ship rolling badly. She
was of course scratch armed, so was quite light, but it
was probably the light winds and heavy seas that
were responsible for this behaviour as Eliza recorded

A typical shipbuilding draught of the period. Dated for a survey of 1796 of the *Hebe*, it is an instruction to Chatham Royal
Dockyard to build a frigate, possibly HMS *Pomone*. It also carries a note that the drawings for HMS *Surprise*, built at Milford
Dockyard, were recalled and sent to India for HMS *Trincomalee*'s build, the *Java* having been sunk with the original set of
drawings. Further annotation shows Seppings' alterations to bow and stern to be found in HMS *Unicorn*. (© *National Maritime
Museum, Greenwich, London, ZAZ4909*)

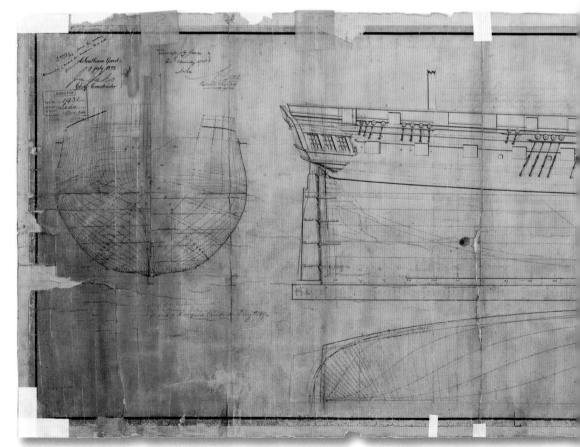

WHY TRINCOMALEE?

Trincomalee was most likely named after the battle of Trincomalee that was fought between the British fleet under Vice-Admiral Sir Edward Hughes and a French fleet under the Bailli de Suffren off the Ceylonese port of Trincomalee on 3 September 1782.

The value of this large natural harbour was first recognised by the Portuguese as a safe haven during the North East monsoons; taken by the Dutch and eventually captured from them by the Royal Navy during the Napoleonic wars it later became part of the Crown Colony of Ceylon.

Used by the Navy for some years during the Dutch occupation as a useful, if occasional, base in which to careen and refit ships (activities which, in those days, needed little in the way of shore facilities). Once in British hands plans were laid for a major base for the Navy. One of the driving factors behind this was the perception that the East India Company was making undue profits from their dealings with the fleet and that things would be cheaper in Ceylon. As it transpired Ceylon lacked many of the basic materials and timber, for example, continued to be imported from India. However with the wars over the need to keep a fleet in being off the Indian coast had passed by the time HMS *Trincomalee* was launched. The building programme for the base was put on hold in 1822 as part of the economies that followed the end of hosilities with France, after a wharf, storehouses and two residences for an Admiral and a Commissioner, neither of whom were ever appointed, had been built. By 1840 there were enough facilities to support a small squadron, and later an ordnance depot and small hospital were established. Although the completion of a dry dock in Colombo on the other side of the island significantly reduced Trincomalee's importance, it survived Admiral Fisher's economies of the early twentieth century and was only finally given up by the Royal Navy in 1957. Today it is a base for the small Sri Lankan navy.

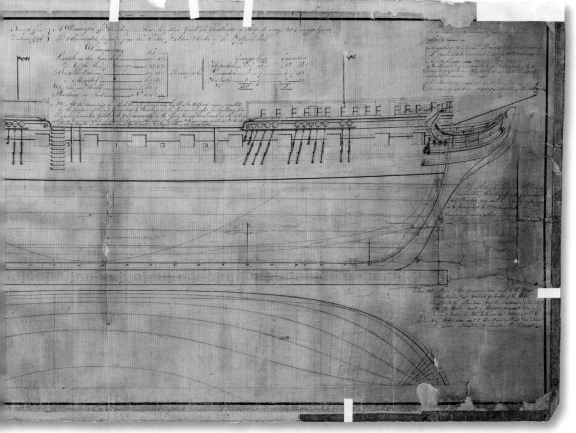

speeds of one knot or less on several occasions.

As built she was a standard 18-pounder frigate, fitted for twenty-eight 18-pounder guns, four nine-pounder cannon and fourteen carronades. Her layout was typical of such vessels, with accommodation for the 320 men needed to handle her rig and man her guns. Her internal layout was equally typical of a large frigate of the day with most of the crew accommodated on the lower deck. This layout shows the clear differentiation between officers, senior rates and junior rates in terms of their allotted areas, with the captain's accommodation on the main deck being greatest of all. Officers and senior rates had cabins, with the officers also having their wardroom, whilst ratings had some fourteen inches of hammock space each. This social distinction is still current in modern warships, although the difference in area allotted is perhaps no longer as marked.

From her diary Eliza seems to have been allocated a cabin for her family, big enough to have cots for her

Captain Richard Laird Warren who commanded *Trincomalee* on her first commission when he was in his mid-30s. This portrait shows him later in life. *(Trincomalee Trust)*

and her children, although not so big that her cot wasn't hitting the table during the worst of the rolling. It is notable that she seemed very reluctant to set foot on the quarter deck without invitation. The social distinction clearly still applied even to civilian passengers.

Commander Bridges was an interesting character who had actually served on board HMS *Leda* in 1813 whilst a lieutenant. Much of his service seems to have been in frigates or smaller, although his most noted service was as a midshipman in a cutting out action in 1803. He was an ideal choice for the first master of a new frigate and from Eliza's diary seems to have been a humane man, although there were a few floggings during the voyage, mainly for drunkenness. The most notable event was his marriage to his betrothed, Harriet Young, at Cape Town, having brought her from Mauritius where her father, Colonel Alexander Young was Commissary-General. Their 'honeymoon' was the rest of the voyage home. Bridges is last recorded as promoted to Post-Captain in 1829 and then on half pay.

Trincomalee was intended to be ship rigged, that is with square sails set on each mast, although it is quite possible that the temporary rig used to bring her home was not as designed and in any case it was removed as soon as she arrived.

INTO SERVICE

It is a measure of the qualities of teak that, twenty-six years later, the two Bombay built frigates were considered in such excellent condition that she and her sister *Amphitrite* were both brought out of reserve. Some alterations were made to *Trincomalee*'s structure, with fewer gun ports for the reduced main deck armament and a continuous bulwark giving a much more modern appearance. Her armament changed from the design outfit to twenty-six cannon of which eighteen were 32-pounders, giving her in fact a greater weight of firepower. Her crew was reduced to 240 men as a result of the fewer guns. She was then classed as a 'spar deck or gun deck corvette' and, in 1847, she finally left to take up duties on the North America and West Indies station under Captain Richard Warren.

In the years since *Trincomalee*'s launch the Royal Navy had changed considerably and whilst not yet a fully modernised service was at least in the process of leaving behind 'rum, sodomy and the lash' in favour of a career that was long term with good pay and a pension. Although these reforms would not be fully achieved until April 1853, a year into her second commission, sufficient changes had been achieved which meant a significant element of her crew during the first commission had been trained at the new gunnery school HMS *Excellent*. Equally, a large portion

Colin Baxter's fine watercolour of *Trincomalee* arriving in Portsmouth after her long delivery voyage from her namesake port. *(Courtesy of the artist Colin Baxter)*

were career Royal Navy seamen, many having started as boys in the training establishments set up around the country to improve the lot of the urban poor, a role that *Trincomalee* would eventually fulfil herself.

The North America and West Indies stations stretched from the Arctic to the border of Brazil. Thus the first commission, which lasted until 1850, saw the vessel ranging from Venezuela to Newfoundland during a time of much change. Slavery had been outlawed by many countries; the West Indian sugar production was moving from British free farmers to Cuban slave farms as a direct result of British governmental policies; the United States was seen as the biggest threat to local and possibly world peace, eyeing up Cuba having recently seized Texas and Florida from Spain; Venezuela

was in turmoil as coffee prices crashed; the French fisheries off Newfoundland were in direct conflict with the British, and France itself was in the throes of another political upheaval. All this resulted in *Trincomalee* being in great demand, showing the flag, supporting British interests, and those of Spain, and keeping potential trouble makers in their place.

It is of interest to reflect on the changing shades of perceived threat and interest during this period. Britain was possibly leading the world in the fight against slavery, for example, but the act of freeing West Indian slaves led to the Spanish slave farms on Cuba undercutting the prices of West Indian sugar, whilst British tax protection had been lifted and credit restrictions imposed, which all combined to drive many British

21

farmers and newly freed slaves out of business. At the same time a perceived threat to Cuba from the USA, which had gobbled up Spanish territories on the American mainland, was seen as contrary to our interests requiring frequent flag showing visits to Cuba, thus protecting the very farms that were putting ours out of work.

Despite frequent denials, it seems that the USA was as imperialist as any other predominantly 'European' country of the period and their expansionist policies were seen by many as a real threat; it was still within living memory, for example, that they had invaded Canada. This potential threat led to an almost continuous upgrading of the defences of Bermuda, being one of only two fortified bases on this station, the other being Halifax in Nova Scotia.

Many of the other port visits were made directly to support British investments or trade, some of which

Trincomalee's commander during her second commission, Captain Wallace Houston, here photographed as an Admiral, probably around 1877. He was a successful commander, somewhat more modern in his outlook than his predecessor. (*Trincomalee Trust*)

reached significant sizes. Trade with Venezuela, for example, was of the order of one million pounds per annum. Other visits, which would be described as 'Aid to the Civil Power' today, took place in the aftermath of hurricanes or earthquakes to help make good damage for example.

Off Newfoundland the duty was mainly that of Fishery Protection, intervening in disputes between French and Newfoundland fishing boats and keeping an eye out for French smugglers.

All these duties would have been recognised by RN warship crews until relatively recently, and indeed are probably still in the job descriptions of the vessels of the much reduced twenty-first century fleet, if they could but find the time for them.

Captain Warren went on to command HMS *Cressy*,

The sister ships HMS *Amphitrite* and *Trincomalee*, both Bombay-built, seen here leaving San Francisco. Judging by the other vessel present they have just dropped a pilot, the large number on the vessel's sail indicating a pilot schooner of the day. This watercolour is dated 23 September 1854, so it is possible the frigates have been examining ships bound for Russia. (© *National Maritime Museum, Greenwich, London, PAH0799*)

a screw third rate, 80-gun, ship-of-the-line. His time in command took in the Russian War, and won *Cressy* the battle honours Baltic 1854-1855. Subsequently he was promoted to Rear-Admiral and took over as Commander-in-Chief, South East Coast of America, the area where he had been active in *Trincomalee*. His last posting, on promotion to Vice-Admiral, was as Commander-in-Chief, the Nore, flying his flag in HMS *Pembroke*, and he is recorded as having retired from this post in April 1870.

Trincomalee's next commission would take her to the far side of the world. Her armament was once

again modernised and she was fitted with ten 32-pounder cannon, ten eight-inch shell guns and one ten-inch shell gun, then the Navy's largest piece of ordnance, but with no change to the size of the crew. She was commissioned for the Pacific Squadron in 1852 under the command of Captain Wallace Houstoun, leaving Plymouth on 21 August.

This final commission took her across the broad expanses of the Pacific Ocean from Valparaiso to Port Clarence in Alaska (now a US Coast Guard station); from Tahiti to the Kamchatka Peninsula, with frequent visits to the Sandwich Islands (modern Hawaii). At the

Trincomalee drying her sails. This is believed to be in Honolulu although the picture offers little clue from the background; the small boat in the foreground could well be from the Hawaiian islands. *(Courtesy H L Chase Bishop Museum, Honolulu, Hawaii)*

conclusion of her five-year deployment she had covered over 110,000 miles, and spent at least half her time at sea.

During this period the Crimean war, or more accurately the Russian War (1853-56), both started and finished, and although briefly involved in the expedition to Petropavlovsk, most of *Trincomalee*'s contacts with the Russians were amicable. These included a visit to the capital of Russian Alaska at Sitka where Prince Albert's birthday was jointly celebrated with the anniversary of Tsar Nicholas II's coronation in August 1853. In fact news of the war did not reach the Pacific until late 1854. Alaska did not become part of the

USA until 1867, ten years after *Trincomalee*'s return home. Oddly enough, the impetus behind its sale by Russia was the fear that it might have been lost to the British during the Russian War. The sale would have gone through earlier but for the American Civil War (1861-1865).

In the Pacific, as in the Atlantic, American expansionism featured strongly and, in the case of the Pacific, the apparent target was Hawaii. *Trincomalee* was to make several visits to Oahu where the Royal Navy was based and whilst there Houstoun surveyed and described the harbour at Pearl Harbour. In between visits *Trincomalee* was at one point to be found anchored off Alcatraz in San Francisco Bay to stop any Russian or American ships taking supplies to Russian Territory. One wonders what the US Navy would make of a similar event today.

Other ports of call included the Pitcairn Islands, where she anchored in Bounty Bay, Tahiti and Peru; but more often the new colony of Esquimalt, the foundation stone of the colony of British Columbia.

Captain Wallace Houstoun, like her first master, had experience with frigates and with Bombay-built ships. Before coming to *Trincomalee* he had served as a Lieutenant on the Bombay-built frigate *Madagascar* and had then commanded the Bombay-built depot ship *Imaum* under Commodore Alexander Sharpe. His last command was a five month appointment in HMS *Orion*. Houstoun retired in 1877 with the rank of Admiral, but seems to have held no commands after *Orion*.

Esquimalt harbour, a view dated c1860. The vessel on the left is the *Trincomalee*, whilst the other vessels could be merchant ships as they lack the white line along their hulls. *(Trincomalee Trust)*

4|TRAINING SHIP

POST-SERVICE CAREER

At the end of her second commission on 3 September 1857 *Trincomalee* was once again laid up in ordinary. In fact the decision had already been made that pure sailing ships could no longer serve in the Royal Navy's wartime fleets. However *Trincomalee* was still in such good condition that she was saved from sale out of service or demolition. In 1860 the decision was taken to use her as a training ship for the Royal Naval Reserve, an organisation which had recently been formalised by the 1859 Naval Reserve Act.

Whilst there had been training ships of various organisations around Britain's coast for some time, most were designed to take disadvantaged boys (to use a modern term) at around eleven or twelve years of age and give them a future of some sort. Of course the basic intention was to provide a good supply of men for the Royal Navy, always in need in times of war, but many also went into the merchant marine and a few found their metier in the trades associated with a seagoing life. The leading charity in this field was the Marine Society, founded in 1756 by Jonas Hanway and still in being today, albeit with updated intentions. According to the Marine Society's website Hanway was concerned that the King's Navy did not press his crews as he was for the poor of the land. Be that as it may, the success of the venture was obvious with a claimed significant portion of the manpower at Trafalgar having come from the Society. This success attracted its emulators with thirty-odd training vessels from a variety of organisations being set up around the coast.

The Navy's intentions for the Naval Reserve were somewhat different. The idea was to retain a pool of skilled men who were up to date with modern naval equipment and tactics who could be called upon in times of strife. Although not used since 1814 this act finally put an end to the need for impressment. Like the training ships the Reserve took lads, but older, at fifteen or sixteen and trained them from scratch. Later the Reserve would also include men who had served, were still under an obligation to serve, and whose skills were kept up to date by the Reserve.

Her initial base was to be Sunderland and she was fitted with modern 32-pounder cannon and eight-inch shell guns to train the reservists. She served first as a tender to the existing drill ship HMS *Castor* before being made a separate command and moving to Hartlepool in 1862. She remained at Hartlepool until paid off in 1872, having had six commanding officers during her time as a drill ship. She was then modified to take some of the Navy's latest guns, the seven-inch rifled muzzleloaders. In 1877 she was towed to Southampton to resume training duties for a further 18 years, under five further commanding officers. Replaced by HMS *Medea* in 1895 she was finally paid off and sold for breaking in May 1897.

GEOFFREY WHEATLEY COBB

Enter Geoffrey Wheatley Cobb, a philanthropist, whose home was Caldicot Castle and who had a comfortable income from a share in the South Wales coalfield in the Rhondda Valley. Cobb apparently had a passion for things maritime and was clearly aware of the various

A sketch by Geoffrey Cobb, dated 1902, of the *Trincomalee* under all plain sail, but labelled as *Foudroyant II*. The date is after Cobb had purchased *Trincomalee* as a replacement for his wrecked *Foudroyant*, but appears to show *Trincomalee* as she was in Royal Navy service. *(Trincomalee Trust)*

Boys and young men training on *Foudroyant*, hauling in a cannon. The sign, 'Remember Nelson', is now exhibited on a deck beam on the gun deck. *(© National Maritime Museum, Greenwich, London, P39147)*

charities using former warships as a foundation for improving the lot of the poor.

His first training ship was Nelson's one time Mediterranean flagship, HMS *Foudroyant*. This vessel had been built in Devonport and launched in 1798; she had been named after the captured French vessel, taken into the Navy as HMS *Foudroyant* in December 1758, which had served with some distinction until 1787, being present at the Battle of Ushant and the relief of Gibraltar.

When Cobb came across the British-built ship in 1892 she had already been partially dismantled and he had to rebuild a considerable part of her upper hull and all of the masting and rigging. His intention was to sail her around the coast as a working ship, training boys for the sea. Unfortunately he misjudged both the

The restored HMS *Foudroyant*, probably at the conclusion of Cobb's rebuild at Cowes, Isle of Wight. *(Trincomalee Trust)*

Trincomalee as *Foudroyant* seen in a dry dock, possibly at the conclusion of her rebuild, with the additions to the poop and forecastle, but without the additional boat davits with which she was later fitted. *(Trincomalee Trust)*

effort needed to man a large square rigged ship and the dangers of a lee shore with the result that she was driven ashore at Blackpool and wrecked in June 1897. Contemporary photographs of the wreck show the new upperworks had been demolished by the prover-bial loose cannon, leading to a suspicion that she had not been very solidly rebuilt.

Undeterred Cobb was now in need of a replace-ment ship and the Admiralty suggested he approach the purchasers of *Trincomalee*, Read's Shipbreakers. So doing he managed to secure the ship for his scheme, renaming her *Foudroyant* after her predecessor, effec-tively eclipsing the name *Trincomalee* for several generations.

After completing the purchase Cobb had her towed to Cowes on the Isle of Wight, where she spent the next five years being fitted out for his service. Additions to the vessel included a new poop deck, cabin, bath-rooms and heads on the fo'c'sle thus altering her profile and in this state she was to remain until restora-tion in the 1990s. During the forty years or so that Cobb himself ran the ship she travelled from Cowes to Falmouth, to Milford Haven, back to Falmouth and then back to Milford Haven. It was during the last spell

in Falmouth that Cobb, looking to expand, took on the *Implacable*, the former *Duguay-Trouin* of France, but it was not until after his death in 1931 that the two ships were reunited in Portsmouth, where they remained until 1949.

Before his death Cobb had signed over *Implacable* to a managing committee responsible for maintaining the vessel. After his death his widow was advised to sign over *Foudroyant* to the Implacable Committee and move the vessels to Portsmouth in 1932 where training continued until the outbreak of the Second World War.

During this time the emphasis changed from the rescue of destitute boys to adventure training for both boys and girls, often referred to the ships by schools, parents and the Sea Scouts. It is recorded that some 10,000 youngsters passed through the ships over the seven years up to the outbreak of war, when all training was suspended except for Sea Scouts and in 1940 both ships were offered to the Navy. Initially used as store ships in 1943 they were returned to the training role under the name HMS *Foudroyant*, providing signalling and seamanship instruction for new entrants.

In this 1972 photograph *Foudroyant*'s poop deck cabin and gallery can clearly be seen above the original stern gallery. This photo also shows her fine lines which contributed to the *Leda* classes' reputation for being fine sailers, but also led to a smaller hull volume, a constant source of complaint. *(Photo: Jonathan Eastland / Ajax)*

POST-SECOND WORLD WAR

Before the end of the war the committee sat to decide the future training programme and the future of the ships. A result of these deliberations that *Implacable* met her fate, a victim of straitened circumstances as much as anything. On being quoted a sum necessary for restoration the committee were forced to decline her return from the Navy and, all else failing, she was ceremonially scuttled flying the flags of Britain and France. *Foudroyant* was in better condition and by 1947 the committee had resolved to continue the training programme and renamed itself the Foudroyant Committee.

This training was to continue until the mid-1980s, latterly under the auspices of the Foudroyant Trust, until it became obvious the vessel needed some work, and at the same time the Portsmouth Historic Dockyard was being formed. For various reasons *Foudroyant* was not considered to add anything to this and the Trustees thoughts turned to long term restoration as the frigate she originally was. For the full details of the various *dramatis personae* involved and the deliberations held the reader is referred to Andrew Lambert's book *Trincomalee: The Last of Nelson's Frigates.*

TS *FOUDROYANT* MEMORIES

It must have been early 1970s when I first went on board *Foudroyant* in Portsmouth Harbour, as a pupil from Lee-on-the-Solent Junior School. I knew not what to expect, other than that we were to sleep in hammocks. My father, a PO in the Navy, cut an old broomstick in half, put notches in the ends and told me they were 'stretchers for my hammock cords' and duly packed them in my kit bag. They did not last long. Upon boarding the ship, which I had often seen from a distant Gosport ferry, we were shown our places below and our hook numbers for our hammocks, boys one side, girls the other. I proudly produced my bits of broomstick.

'Where did you get those?' roared the Bosun. 'If I see them again they are going straight over the side!'

It is strange the memories that come back to you. One was definitely the smell. I don't know what was used to scrub down the heads, galley and mess deck, but I guess it was some pungent mix of bleach and carbolic. Secondly, I remember my hammock. Whether just poorly strung, or deliberately given me by a grumpy Bosun who had 'his eye on me', I recall that it curled up like a cocoon or a half open peapod, no matter what I did to correct it. If there was 'trouble' or too much talking in hammocks, we were sent on deck in the cold dead of night. I can't remember what I had done, but the deck at night in the middle of Portsmouth harbour was a scary place for a young boy.

Life afloat for our short stay was divided between daily chores and activities. I seemed to have got out of the early scrubbing and the making of breakfast. Being a big lad and trusted by my teachers, I was one of two sent off in the blue tender with a uniformed crewman in the mornings, berthing at the ferry pontoon and then marching up a deserted High Street to fetch the bread and post. My mates thought I had the easy job.

We did get afloat in boats too, both rowing and sailing craft. I'd never rowed a big boat before. We splashed and pulled and splashed some more. Looking back, I'm not sure we were ever untied from our mooring buoy. We also sailed on a small yacht, so many packed in that I could see barely anything, let alone know what was going on as sheets were pulled in or let fly, and sails slatted and banged above us as we heeled over, coats pulled up within huge lifejackets to keep out spray, wind and rain.

I'd always had an interest in history, which is probably why I liked the old vessel with its cannons on deck, and I recall that we were taken deep within the ship, and shown a rolled-up length of dirty canvas, 'This was HMS *Victory*'s topsail at Trafalgar'. Nobody else has ever confirmed this but, of course, it hangs on display today in the Museum next to *Victory*. Perhaps it was just some old awning, with a good yarn added to inspire young boys.

In later years I went aboard again for the summer fairs. A boat ride from the Gosport Ferry pontoon brought visitors to the old *Foudroyant*, all 'en-fete', bedecked with her flags fluttering in a stiff harbour breeze. Mementos such as pennants and badges were for sale, and there was that smell again.

Though the ship has now left the harbour for a better life in Hartlepool, I can look out on her old moorings from my Royal Clarence Yard Studio and recall her presence where modern yachts now lie. I expect that in an old Gosport bosun's shed there's still a drum or two of that cleaning stuff, just in case she returns.

Colin M Baxter, Marine Artist

5 | RESTORATION

HARTLEPOOL HAD BEEN INSTRUMENTAL IN THE restoration of HMS *Warrior*, a task that had finished in 1987, leaving them free to take on another such project. Teesside Development Corporation's financial support and Portsmouth Historic Dockyard's disdain made the choice of Hartlepool a foregone conclusion. The team assembled all had *Warrior* experience, albeit with an iron ship, although as she had some 355 tons of teak as backing to her armour, she probably had more teak in her than *Trincomalee*.

On 28 March 1990 it was announced that she would revert to her original name HMS *Trincomalee* and shortly afterwards the Foudroyant Trust was made dormant and the HMS Trincomalee Trust was formed with the same trustees.

The vessel was initially berthed at the old coal dock, all evidence of which had been razed and which was later to become the site of a small hotel. Lambert describes the scene as one of 'almost apocalyptic post-industrial decline' and indeed the author on his first visit had a great deal of trouble reconciling the surroundings with his grandfather's career in colliers, shipping coal from Hartlepool to Limehouse Basin for the best part of 30 years. Since the vessel's completion her surroundings have changed beyond all recognition and for the better. Hartlepool Borough Council has clearly been very active in regenerating the town and its surroundings.

On her arrival various negotiations were necessary with all the potential stakeholders and funders of the restoration. The reader is referred to Andrew Lambert's book for a blow-by-blow account of the behind the scenes work so necessary and yet often so convoluted. To highlight just one minor issue, relating to the National Register of Historic Vessels, *Trincomalee* would have been excluded as she had not been built in the UK. This situation was speedily resolved and the criteria have since been changed to include ships of UK design, wherever built. At the time, however, this added some unneeded angst to the proceedings.

One other, more major, issue which could have had a direct effect on the restoration process was that of the dry dock. This had been filled in at some stage in the past and its restoration was to take longer than anticipated. Thus the restoration of the *Trincomalee* was initially carried out afloat, leaving the timbers below the waterline to be dealt with when the dock eventually became available. Whilst not an ideal situation, in retrospect it seems to have done little to hold up the restoration.

Work therefore started with the vessel secured

Captain David Smith,
OBE FNI RN, 1927-2013

Captain David Smith had a long and distinguished career in the Royal Navy and Trinity House.

In 1976 he was appointed Chairman of The *Foudroyant* Trust, later the HMS *Trincomalee* Trust. He was dedicated to the objective of restoring *Trincomalee* to her former glory and oversaw the detailed work of restoration ensuring repair and replacement work was carried out correctly. Under his chairmanship, the Trust raised more than £10.5million for this work over eleven years.

His efforts were recognised by his appointment as OBE, by the World Ship Trust's personal award in 2001 and by the award of a Society for Nautical Research Victory medal in 2011.

alongside. The additions gained in Cowes were stripped off, as were the additions and alterations made since 1845, much of which were of surprisingly poor quality. By removing most of her solid ballast she was sufficiently far out of the water to enable much of the sides to be dealt with, the rotten or damaged woodwork being stripped back to intact timbers. African opepe was used to replace the unsound timbers, teak being expensive and difficult to obtain, and the vessel was rebuilt up to the original bulwarks. It had been decided to retain the 1845 stern alterations. These were found to be completely sound once the false poop had been stripped off. Otherwise the Trust intended to return her to the appearance she would have had if finished and rigged as designed in 1817.

This decision involved re-aligning the gun ports, designing and manufacturing masts, spars and rigging from scratch and fitting out the completed ship with all the paraphernalia of an in-service warship of the period.

One of the major problems faced by any warship preservation group of any era is the size of the staff available to look after the restored ship. It has to be remembered that during the history of warships the vessel was always manned to fight the ship. In addition to those needed simply to run the vessel there was always a number of men doing very little until called on to fight. It is quite probable that every captain has attempted to solve the problem of 'idle hands' in the same way, with 'hands to paint ship' being as familiar to Nelson's navy as it was to the crew of the last generation of steam frigates and destroyers. This abundance of labour is rarely available to a preservation trust, so some of the decisions made at this point reflected a common sense approach to long-term maintenance.

This is well demonstrated by the decision to replicate the masts and spars in rolled steel sections and to ultimately use modern man-made fibres for the cordage.

Equally it would have been short-sighted to stress the restored structure by mounting actual cannon weighing around 2.5 tons on their carriage, so replica barrels were made from fibre-glass.

The work progressed steadily through the early 1990s until August 1996 when the dock was finally ready to receive her. Once docked down a survey of the underwater hull was possible and it was found to be sound except for the wind and water area, that is the part of the hull which is alternately exposed to the air and immersed in water. This is always a source of concern because of the mixed environment. In *Trincomalee*'s case this area was found to need large-scale restoration as is frequently the case with elderly vessels of any construction, wood or iron.

Work on this area continued throughout 1998 and culminated with the restoration of the coppering. A 'copper bottom' refers to the advantage gained by British ships once the ship had been sheathed in copper plate. This was the solution eventually adopted to protect a ship's underwater planking from attack by boring worms and from the attachment of marine growth which would significantly slow a ship down, particularly one spending time in tropical waters. The copper was nailed in place, with copper nails, over a layer of tarred felt, to minimise any possible electrolytic impact on the iron bolts and nails used in the hull structure. Historically such fastenings were rapidly replaced with copper bolts once the problem had been encountered. *Trincomalee* was fully re-coppered in a near authentic fashion during her time in dock and by May 2000 she was once again afloat.

After some more convolutions the museum and replica Georgian quayside you see today were built around the ship as a visitor centre. It was an early decision that such a centre would be necessary, in part to reduce the amount of interpretation material needed on board. Excessive display boards were thought, rightly, to detract from the authentic atmosphere of a Georgian warship in all counts ready for sea.

A fine winter's afternoon in Hartlepool. *Trincomalee*, beautifully restored and in her dock, has to contend with a harsher climate very different to that her original timbers knew when building, in Bombay. *(© Christopher Armstrong)*

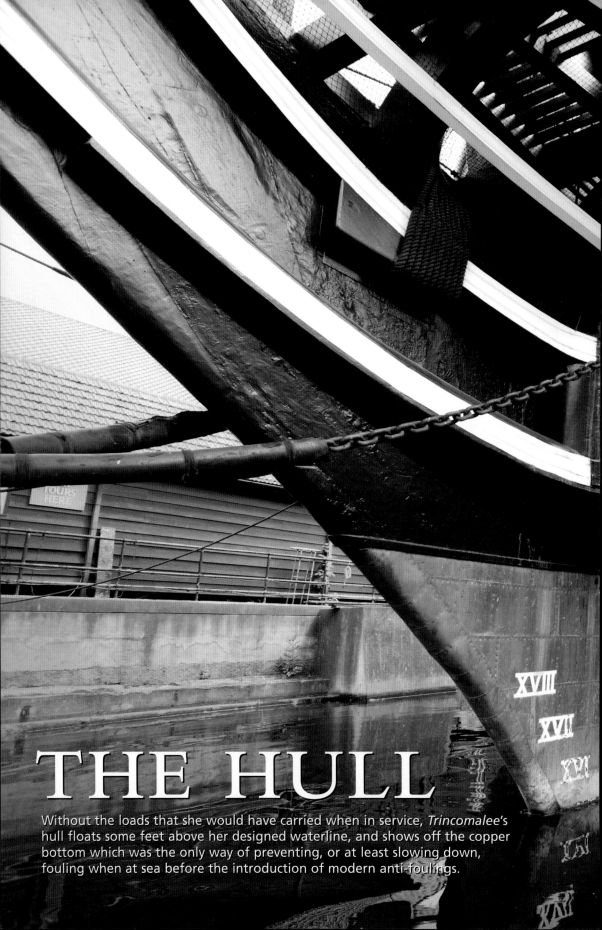

THE HULL

Without the loads that she would have carried when in service, *Trincomalee*'s hull floats some feet above her designed waterline, and shows off the copper bottom which was the only way of preventing, or at least slowing down, fouling when at sea before the introduction of modern anti-foulings.

The epitome of the Nelsonic era frigate, *Trincomalee* rests in the Jackson Dock in Hartlepool. Other than the modern weather cloths on the main deck, the view seen by today's visitor would not have been unfamiliar to our forebears whenever a warship was docked for repairs or refit.

The frigate of this era had one continuous deck, the quarterdeck and the forecastle being structurally a single plane with the waist – the length of deck in the centre where there are no bulwarks – linking the two areas fore and aft. The clean sweep of the deck was needed for the handling of the sails and boats and, when in action, for firing cannon and carronades. Below this level is the gun deck, or upper deck, that level indicated by the white paint, and this deck carried the main armament. Below that, roughly at the level of the waterline, can be found the mess deck, or lower deck, where the crew

lived. There were no guns on this deck because its closeness to the water precluded having any gun ports or scuttles. Below the waterline are the orlop deck and the hold.

Research carried out on the carpenter's returns from HMS *Victory* seem to leave little doubt that the selected colours truly reflect the period in question. The green was known as 'longboat green' and the gun ports were painted 'gun port maroon', a colour that was originally introduced aboard warships to disguise the blood of battle. The decks were left unpainted and kept tight – watertight – by the daily application of seawater when scrubbing them and from the water and spray that the vessel shipped during spells of hard weather at sea. Pine-derived tar, sourced from northern Europe, was the main substance applied to the ship's hull and was a fine preservative against rot.

This view from above gives a good idea of the upper deck layout, from the two cannon, the bitts at the base of the foremast, the belfry with the ship's bell between the two forward companionways on the forecastle, the mainmast, capstan head, binnacle with the compasses, steering wheels, mizzen mast and all surrounded by the cannon and carronades on the quarterdeck. The deck was arranged for twelve guns, six each 32-pounder carronades and 18-pounder cannon, leaving some gun ports vacant for ease of circulation.

Also clearly visible are two of the purpose-built fixed fenders against which the ship is moored, again matched by a similar arrangement on the other side, and the mooring lines, all required when the wind pipes up.

Trincomalee has been restored to her 1817 condition with the exception of the stern that had been modified in 1845 when she was converted to a sloop, or gun deck corvette, and given an elliptical stern. However, it retains very much the look of the traditional square stern of frigates built at the turn of the century, with the stern gallery windows dominating the picture, giving light to the captain's cabin, and with quarter galleries either side.

One of the most vulnerable parts of the Napoleonic warship was this stern. Glass, along with the light wood framework, provided absolutely no protection against cannon balls, and the few internal bulkheads not much more, presenting an enemy with the opportunity to rake the gun deck, usually putting a large number of the ship's own guns out of action and killing and maiming gun crews. The round or circular stern, introduced in the 1820s, and which can be seen today on HMS *Unicorn* in Dundee (see page 12), was intended to increase the strength of this traditionally weak part of the ship and enhance its defence against raking fire.

Left: The view of the stern shows the davits for the 18ft cutter, otherwise known as the jolly boat, which was the smallest of the ship's boats and used for a variety of general purpose tasks, as well as the stern lights and the modern mooring chains. Just visible are the outer ends of the two hawse pipes leading into the captain's cabin though which mooring lines would be run.

Right: The gilded initials GR, George Rex.

Below: Close-up views of individual components of the stern decoration, or gingerbread as it was often called. The elephant is a reference to the ship's place of build, and is correctly shown as an Indian elephant, while flowers and garlands complete the ensemble.

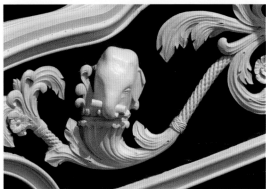

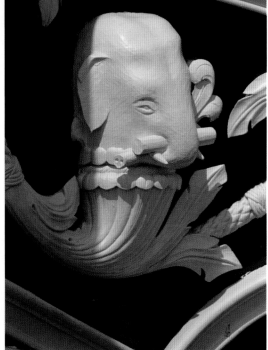

Left and right: The decoration below the quarter gallery is replicated on the starboard side. The detail of the end of the frieze at the top of the quarter gallery.

Far right: Frigates had two octagonal navigation lanterns fitted on the taffrail at the stern.

Far right centre: One of the six delicate garlands that decorate the external stern timbers. These stern timbers, or counter timbers as they are sometimes referred to, that framed the large lights (windows) were a weak point in the ship.

Far right bottom: The stopper in the stern gallery hawse pipe seen from outboard which prevented the ingress of water when the ship was at sea.

A port side view of the stern gallery and the port quarter gallery. The green windows in the quarter gallery represent the non-glazed areas around the Captain's and officers' latrines, or 'seats of easement' as they were known. Above is the port davit for the ship's boat. Davits fitted at the transom above the stern lights was common practice by the time of *Trincomalee*.

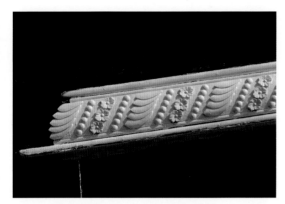

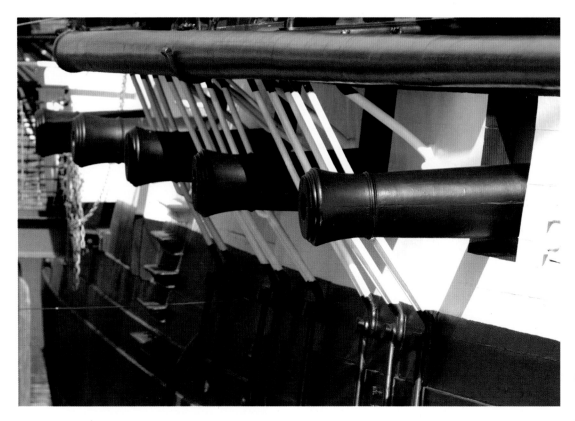

Above: A view of the port side main armament showing the positions of the cannon when run out for action, relative to the channel taking the shrouds (above). Careful positioning of the channels in relation to the gunports was crucial so that the chain plates that carried the strain of the shrouds did not get in the way of the cannon. The spar is a stunsail boom stowed against the channel.

Below: Part of the ship's copper bottom. The copper sheets were attached to the hull over a layer of tarred cloth, and formed an effective anti-fouling measure that gave the Royal Navy a notable tactical edge when first introduced in the latter decades of the eighteenth century. A speed advantage of up to 2-3 knots could be expected, boring by the Teredo navalis worm was much reduced, and fouling by marine growth took far longer, meaning less time was spent in dock.

Below: The frigate was one of the largest ships expected to be rowed by its crew. This is a typical oar, or sweep, port to be found along the length of the gun deck. The ports were hinged from forward, with a horseshoe shaped hinge, and secured from within. Oars represented very much an auxiliary form of motive power, and their purpose was largely tactical: manoeuvering in confined waters, in very light winds, or after heavy damage aloft. Their use had long been a matter of debate even at the time of *Trincomalee*'s construction and by the time she was finally commissioned, thirty years later, they had largely been superseded as an auxiliary source of power by the new steam engine, which within another decade would be supplanting masts and sails too.

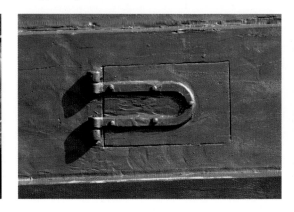

Left and above: The port cathead, the bracket to which the anchor was fixed when not in use. First recorded in the 1620s, the ends were richly carved, usually with the head of a lion. This was a separate piece of timber and, as well as being decorative, it also prevented wet from entering and rotting the end grain of the timber beam. Three sheaves in slots were part of the tackle with which the anchor was pulled up to the cathead. In this position the anchor was said to be 'catted'.

Below: A fine view of the main anchor, seized up to the cathead. This view also shows the closeness of the cannon to the anchor, the forward 18-pounder having a very restricted training arc.

XVIII

Above: The ship's bow showing the anchor chain leading to the forward hawse holes. Also clearly visible are the present-day mooring lines and chains which hold *Trincomalee* in position in her dock.

Left and below: A feature of this end of a sailing warship was the placing of the crew's 'seat of easement', or latrine, in the ship's head, thus the term 'heads' which has come down into modern usage. They were fitted on a small deck forward of the beakhead bulkhead, in this case one either side of the bowsprit and, as can be seen, they drain directly into the sea.

THE FIGUREHEAD

Figureheads were a feature of most warships of this era, except perhaps for the very smallest. In fact figureheads are part of a tradition that goes back many centuries, to ancient Greece at least. In the case of the Royal Navy, their use finally died out during the early decades of the twentieth century; the last ship built with one being the sloop Espiegle, launched at Sheerness in 1900 and only sold out of service in 1923. Hand carved from wood, probably oak or elm, until the Admiralty ordered softwood to be used in the mid-eighteenth century, warships tended to have something with a meaning drawn from the ship's name, although the very biggest had royal coats of arms (for example HMS *Victory*) at their prow. Full figures were abolished at the end of the eighteenth century and they were replaced with busts or half figures.

Until the middle of the eighteenth century figureheads were often gilded but this practice died out and paint was introduced; this saved money and gave better protection against the elements.

Above and left: *Trincomalee's* figurehead is a painted bust and was carved by a member of the famous Hellyer family of ship carvers who produced many figureheads for the Admiralty. This depiction of an Indian with his turban has been identified with her builder, although the figure is clearly not in Parsi dress.

The present figurehead is a recent replica, the original having finally succumbed to some rot; but, remarkably, it had been in place since 1819 until the ship's restoration in the 1990s. It is stored in the museum awaiting restoration.

Prominent in this view of *Trincomalee* taken from ahead are the figurehead, headrails, the catted anchors and hawse holes as well as her coppering and the heavy timbers of the stem and cutwater. A good view of the steeve (angle) of the bowsprit shows it to be around 30 degrees, a common angle throughout this era.

Far left: The fixed boarding ladder on the starboard side. There was another on the port side, and they allowed access to the gun deck from a jetty or boat alongside. These steps are simply timbers fixed to the side of the ship, with no hand holds though ropes were aften lowered each side of the step to make climbing easier.

Left: An iron chainplate or preventer link with two fastenings, taking the loads from the shrouds around the channel into the hull. The opening next to it is a scupper drain.

Below: A general view of the starboard side of *Trincomalee* showing the guns run out for action along the whole length of the gun deck. In the foreground is the best bower anchor catted up to the cathead. The spar seen aft of this almost as a continuation of the anchor stock is in fact a stun sail boom stowed against the channel of the foremast.

Right: Draught marks at the stem. Roman numerals continued to be used for this purpose until 1972 when they were changed to Arabic numerals.

Below right: The stern draught marks. When compared with the waterline at the bow it is evident that the ship is trimmed by the stern by six inches, the space between the six-inch-high figures. The rudder is fixed to the ship using pintles (once called a 'pintail') fixed to the rudder which had at their fore end a pin that fitted into the ring or eye of the gudgeons, which were attached to the ship. The ring just visible above the pintle could have emergency steering chains attached to it.

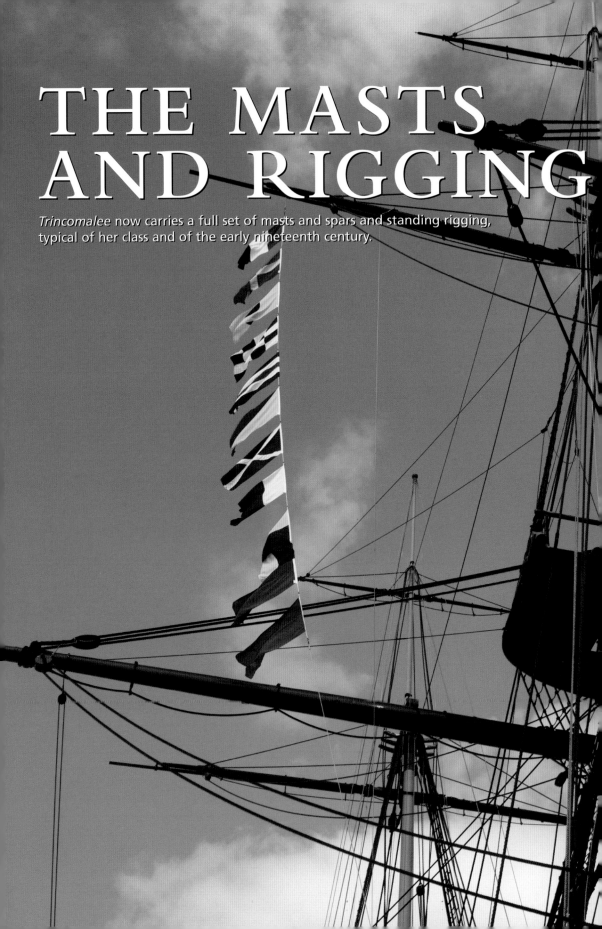

THE MASTS
AND RIGGING

Trincomalee now carries a full set of masts and spars and standing rigging, typical of her class and of the early nineteenth century.

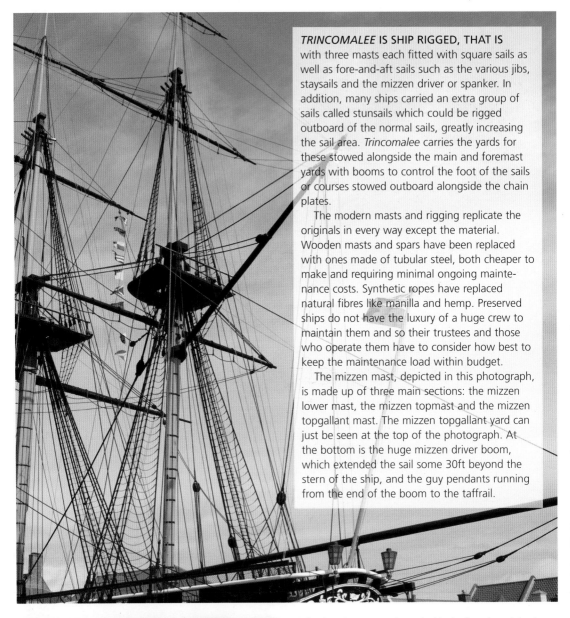

TRINCOMALEE IS SHIP RIGGED, THAT IS with three masts each fitted with square sails as well as fore-and-aft sails such as the various jibs, staysails and the mizzen driver or spanker. In addition, many ships carried an extra group of sails called stunsails which could be rigged outboard of the normal sails, greatly increasing the sail area. *Trincomalee* carries the yards for these stowed alongside the main and foremast yards with booms to control the foot of the sails or courses stowed outboard alongside the chain plates.

The modern masts and rigging replicate the originals in every way except the material. Wooden masts and spars have been replaced with ones made of tubular steel, both cheaper to make and requiring minimal ongoing maintenance costs. Synthetic ropes have replaced natural fibres like manilla and hemp. Preserved ships do not have the luxury of a huge crew to maintain them and so their trustees and those who operate them have to consider how best to keep the maintenance load within budget.

The mizzen mast, depicted in this photograph, is made up of three main sections: the mizzen lower mast, the mizzen topmast and the mizzen topgallant mast. The mizzen topgallant yard can just be seen at the top of the photograph. At the bottom is the huge mizzen driver boom, which extended the sail some 30ft beyond the stern of the ship, and the guy pendants running from the end of the boom to the taffrail.

Left: The mizzen mast channel with the four shroud deadeyes and lanyards attached and, in the centre, the topmast shroud. The spar seen below the channel is the tip of the main mast stunsail boom.

Right: The mizzen mast seen from starboard aft. From the top the three yards are the topgallant yard, topsail yard and the crossjack, pronounced 'crowjack'. The fore and aft spars are the gaff, and just visible behind the lantern, the driver boom. The block in the foreground is at the end of the vang pendant which could be hardened up to prevent the gaff sagging to leeward. The original ropework would have been painted black with Stockholm tar to reduce the damage caused by water and ultra violet light to natural fibres.

Above: The driver gaff was a very significant spar and had a number of functions. Here it (and, when rigged, the mizzen driver sail) is held aloft with the peak halliard, seen here leading to the top of the main mast. The lighter lines leading upwards are the mizzen topsail and mizzen topgallant braces.

Left: The jaws of the driver gaff that held it to the mizzen mast. A parrel leading around the front of the mast kept it in place.

Right: The jaws for the driver boom are supported on boom stays and, like the gaff jaws (see opposite page), are held in place by a parrel around the mast. A parrel was usually made up of a rope, attached to each of the jaws, threaded through wooden balls and then encircling the mast.

Above: Close-up of the mizzen fighting top. Note that the lower mast shrouds pass through the top, through a gap known as the lubber's hole. Seamen would always climb onto the top via the futtock shrouds seen to the left of the picture and over the edge of the top, while 'landlubbers' could reach it through the lubber's hole. In action this top would be manned by marine marksmen tasked with picking off the officers on an enemy's deck.

Right: A mouse. This was a large knot of rope acting as a stopper to the mizzen stay collar. The mizzen stay is passed around the mast and its end made up into a collar. The mouse prevents the stay from tightening around the mast, allowing any adjustment to its tension to be made at deck level. This simple arrangement also means that a damaged stay can be removed and replaced relatively easily.

AS THE NAPOLEONIC WARS WENT ON SO THE need for more and more timber gradually exceeded the supply and masts could no longer be made from single pieces of timber. *Trincomalee*'s lower main mast has been restored to represent a built mast, made up from several pieces of timber in the absence of a single spar of the right size. This became the norm for the main and fore masts, later on for mizzen masts too, and later still for some of the larger yards. Clearly visible here are the two cheek pieces, either side of the mast and the iron hoops, known as wooldings, binding the mast components together. This construction resulted in a considerably stronger mast than one fashioned from a single piece of timber.

This view clearly shows the fighting top and the lubber's hole as well as the shrouds and ratlines giving access to it. Just visible are the stunsail yards stowed beside the main and topsail yards. The large rope in the foreground is the mizzen mast forestay.

Above and right: These three views show the main mast forestay at its fastening at deck level. The forestay is of two parts that pass either side of the fore mast on their way forward to the bow where they are fastened either side of the bowsprit. The job of these stays was to transmit the loads from the mast into the heavy timbers of the bow and the massive lashings employed indicate the sort of loads that these stays carried.

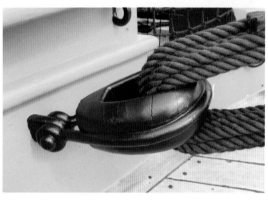

Below: The port main mast channel (with the forward part of the ship to the left), with shrouds coming down to the deadeyes and lanyards and the load being passed through the channel to be taken up by the middle link and then the preventer link, in modern parlance the chain plate, which then takes the load into the hull timbers.

Opposite top: The starboard main channel showing the shrouds, deadeyes and lanyards for tightening up the shrouds. The three holes in each of the deadeyes are the 'eyes', and because they were not fitted with sheaves or pulleys, they were known as 'dead'. The lanyards were always of hemp that stretched less than other material and thus helped to keep the shrouds tight. Also clearly visible is the hinge point for the stunsail boom. The inset shows the small chainplates, set aft of the main channel, for the three main backstays.

Left: A view looking up under the main fighting top. The prominent blocks are taking the foremast main yard braces to the deck below where they are belayed to the fore brace bitts at the foot of the mast. Clearly visible are main stays with their looped ends each held by the rope mouse.

Above: The main topmast cross trees, the three pieces of timber placed athwartships. The two timbers running fore and aft are the trestle trees. Amongst the rigging visible, the largest, which have been looped over the cross trees, are the topmast shrouds. The shrouds here have been wormed, parcelled and served to protect them from chafing. This involves first worming the rope by laying thin pieces of line (worms) between the strands. The rope is then parcelled with strips of canvas, soaked in tar, and finally the canvas is tightly bound (served) with yarn. Resilient to chafe and resistant to water. the shrouds will last far longer than if left uncovered. The yard is the main topsail yard.

Right: The main yard showing the flat wooden battens that reinforce the spar; the cleats with the main jeers, the chains, which are used to raise and lower the spar; the main sling, the heavy rope straps attached via a lanyard to a sling to hold the spar in position; and the truss pendants, the thinner of the ropes, holding the yard tight against the mast.

Above: The main fighting top. This view clearly shows the structure of the platform supported by the two trestle trees either side of the mast, and two elongated cross trees, at the junction of the main and topmasts. Note also the shrouds going through the lubber's hole and the futtock shrouds leading around the top to the topmast shrouds. Also visible is a single rail at the aft edge of the platform. The lifts, the rigging that controlled the horizontal angle of a yard, are the lines heading out of the photograph right and left at 45 degrees.

Below: A close-up of the two main mast stays from forward. Each mouse, knot, prevents the collar of the stay from closing round the mast.

Right: The main topmast. This view looking up at the main topmast from the main top clearly shows the five shrouds and their ratlines, the main topsail yard and its associated stunsail yards, and the main topmast stay and preventer stay, each with its mouse.

Below: The port main brace where it is led back astern from one end of the main yard. With the lower end being fixed, the seamen would haul on the upper end from the deck to brace the main yard round to trim the sails and catch the wind. The phrase to 'splice the main brace' has become the command to issue an extra tot of rum, and is based on the idea that having to repair this rope whilst underway was one of the most difficult jobs for the seaman and thus deserving of reward.

Left: The fore mast. Rigged in an almost identical fashion to the main mast, the fore mast is slightly shorter and the gear correspondingly smaller. Made up of three components, the fore lower mast, the fore topmast and the fore topgallant mast, it has three yards like the main mast. These are the fore lower yard, the fore topsail yard and the fore topgallant yard. Unlike the main mast, its forward stays are taken to the bowsprit and are fitted for various staysails and jibs.

Clearly visible in this view are the stays of the main mast passing either side the fore mast on their way to the bow. Also clearly seen are the foot ropes or horses on each yard; the braces, running aft from the ends of the yards, and the lifts controlling the vertical angles of the yards.

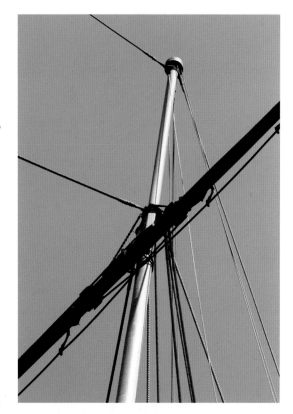

Right: A close-up view of the fore topgallant yard and, above, the truck of the fore mast.

Below: The foremast channel with the attendant shrouds, dead eyes, lanyards and links. Note how the spacing of the shrouds has been arranged around the gun ports. Once again the large boom is a stunsail lower boom in its stowed position.

The sailor's view looking up from the fighting top on the fore mast to the cross trees some 100ft from the deck. The topmasts, unlike the heavier lower masts, were made from single lengths of timber and consequently had no wooldings.

Above: The fore topgallant yard showing the foot ropes (horses), braces and lifts and slings. The slings are attached over the hounds, an eight square section shaped from the mast which include a sheave for the staysail halyard. Also hanging over the hounds are the topgallant shrouds, whilst the vertical black rope is the main topgallant stay.

Left and below: The fighting top of the fore lower mast and, below it, the cheek pieces on each side of the mast; beyond the forward edge of the fighting top can be spotted the fore stay and fore preventer stay each with its mouse, shown in greater detail below.

Above: The fore mast cross trees and the fore topmast shrouds.

Right and below: The top of the fore main mast and, to the right of the photograph, the foot of the fore topmast. The large shrouds and stays are clearly shown looped over the top of the lower mast, and they have all been wormed, parcelled and served to guard against chafing. The two ropes exiting the picture to the bottom right are the fore stay and fore preventer stay. In the photograph to the left is shown the base of the topmast with its fid, or wedge, passing through the base of the spar holding the topmast in place relative to the lower mast. Removal of the fid allowed the topmast to be lowered. The rope ladder is a modern addition to help with maintenance of the rigging.

THE BOWSPRIT AND ITS ASSOCIATED SPARS IS A
massive assembly measuring more than 100ft in
length. The spar that runs into the bow of the ship is
the bowsprit, beyond that are the jib boom and then
the flying jib boom. Beneath the heel of the flying jib
boom is the dolphin striker through which the inner
and outer martingale stays are led, ropes extending
from the end of the jib boom and flying jib boom back
to the stem of the vessel to prevent the upwards thrust
of the jib booms. Above the dolphin striker is the jack
staff while further aft, at the heel of the jib boom, is
the spritsail yard.

Below left: Looking down from the foremast at the bowsprit
assembly. The fore topmast preventer stay and the fore
topmast stay can be seen leading down to the bees, shaped
blocks of wood fitted at the end of the bowsprit just before
the cap. Also visible are the guys from the jib boom and flying
jib boom and the running rigging around the spritsail yard.

Right and Below: The fore preventer stay and the fore stay
run from the top of the fore lower mast to the end of the
bowsprit. Note the collar cleats and the small splines of wood
used to keep the stay collars in place. The collars are wormed,
parcelled and served against wear.

Above: Where the outboard end of the bowsprit, bees, jib boom, dolphin striker, jack staff and spritsail yard all meet. The bowsprit shrouds and the bobstay, as well as the ends of the two fore stays, are also visible. The fore royal stay and the fore topgallant stay can be spotted at top left, leading diagonally out of the photograph.

Top right and below: Two close-ups of the heel of the jib boom and its attachment to the bowsprit. The ribbed piece is the jib boom saddle and forward of that the sliding saddle. The rope work attaching the jib boom to the bowsprit is known as gammoning, the chain being a modern safety requirement.

Right and far right: The bees with a block supporting them from below. The right hand stay is traditionally the fore topmast preventer stay whilst that on the left is the fore topmast stay. Note the cap with its attachment for the jack staff above and the dolphin striker below.

THE UPPER DECK

The upper deck of *Trincomalee* consists of a quarter deck astern measuring almost half the overall length of the vessel and a shorter fo'c'sle, or forecastle, deck forward, the two connected together by walkways at the waist.

THE UPPER DECK CARRIES TWELVE GUNS, six each of 32-pounder carronades and 18-pounder cannon, alternating along its length. When in commission there would have been more but eight have been omitted to make it easier for visitors to move around the deck. In terms of the colour scheme, research has indicated that the inside of the bulwarks and the ports would have been painted in the 'longboat green' and 'gun port maroon' as illustrated here. The photograph illustrates clearly the view of the captain and officers, standing on the quarter deck to command the sailors handling the ship at sea and during battle.

In contrast to the photograph on the previous pages, which is looking aft along the quarter deck, this view is looking forward towards the walkways at the waist and taking in the skylight over the captain's cabin on the gun deck, the mizzen mast and the wheel, and beyond that the capstan. You can see the difference in size of the displayed shot next to the carronade in the foreground and the cannon to its right.

Above: The stern of *Trincomalee* with her ensign staff mounted in position. This was removed at sea when it would have interfered with the free movement of the driver boom. The white rail at the top of the bulwark is known as the taffrail, the sternmost part, or rim, of a vessel.

Right: The layout of the quarter deck, as seen from the main top. Visible are the upper drumhead of the capstan, just aft of the grating over the original hatchway, two further gratings, the binnacle and compasses, the wheel and then the mizzen mast. The two platforms right aft are temporary modern additions.

Left: One of the two stern lanterns, the only lights shown by vessels of this era. This octagonal form was typical of lamps in the eighteenth century, and a similar design can be found on HMS *Victory*. They were supported on the taffrail by a bracket. When in use it would have been fitted with an oil lamp, probably burning sperm whale oil as this was one of the cleanest lamp oils.

Above: The skylight, positioned just behind the mizzen mast, was intended to give some natural light to the captain's cabin on the gun deck below.

Left: Just forward of the skylight are the mizzen bitts, the port one seen in detail. Sheaves, like those here, were introduced during the eighteenth century for running rigging. Each bitt was finished off with a timberhead for securing lines as well as a horizontal dowel, or belaying pin.

Opposite: Two views of the quarter deck and capstan drumhead with, in the upper shot, two of the capstan bars in place. The capstan consists of the drumhead with a decorated cap and several whelps – projecting ribs that enabled rope to get a good grip – attached to the barrel making up the drum for the rope or hawser below. Note the rope decoration around the top and bottom of the drumhead itself. The capstan was protected against a sudden reversal by a pawl in the base of the lower capstan head. Capstans were powerful and were used for hauling anchor hawsers, lifting ship's boats and heavy gear such as masts and yards.

STEERING THE SHIP

A sailing frigate was steered with a double wheel that controlled the tiller two decks below. Each wheel had ten spokes and handles, and they were connected by the rope drum and mounted on a pair of pedestals. A continuous rope was wound around the drum and the two ends made fast to the ends of the tiller. When extra help was needed beyond the capacity of the men on the wheel, then relieving tackles could be added to the actual tiller.

Although the ship's wheel was the primary means

of steering it was not the sole determinant and the set of the sails had considerable influence, so that once sailing on a course at sea the wheel, and hence the rudder, added only minor corrections. The rudder would come into its own at slower speeds, manoeuvring in or out of harbour, in battle or during bad weather – times when the ship was at its most vulnerable.

Right: This close-up of one of the wheels depicts how it is positioned between the rope drum and the pedestal which holds it in position on the deck.

Below: The continuous rope from the drum passes down through the captain's cabin and then down to the after end of the mess deck where the two ends are attached to the tiller that controls the rudder. The six turns of the rope either side of the brass marker in the upright position indicates that the rudder is centered.

Above right: The binnacle usually contained two compasses by which the helmsmen steered the ship. Between them is a lantern for illumination at night and here is a chimney for the lantern smoke.

Right: One of the two compasses. The helmsmen were required to steer by the compass course he was given, and not by any landmark or star.

Above: The view aft from the port side waist walkway. The gratings covering what is essentially an open gun deck have modern rain protection covering them. The two canvas covers to the modern companionways are also prominent in this shot. The space over the gratings was used to stow the ship's boats and any spare spars that were carried, the latter as seen here.

Left: The main mast seen from aft. This clearly shows the mizzen stay leading from top of the mizzen lower mast to the main mast.

Below: The foremast jeer bitts. The two large ropes with soft eyes and a lanyard to a deck bolt are the main topmast stays. The small black cylinder in the background is the galley chimney.

Above: The main jeer bitts. The ropes shown belayed off the cross beam are the various lifts and jeers from the yards above. The large soft eye visible at the top of the picture is the mizzen stay. Once the sails were bent on then a vast amount of running rigging would be added.

Right: The base of the main mast showing the components of the spare bower anchor fixed firmly to the mast. The anchor has been dismantled with the wooden stock lashed separately on the starboard side of the mast. In the days when it was not unheard of for a vessel to have to cut its anchor cable to facilitate a speedy departure, a spare anchor was crucial.

Above: One of the gun ports on the weather deck with no gun, netted off to meet modern health and safety requirements. Note the eye bolts (top) and the ring bolts (below) for attaching the tackle of a gun carriage when placed at this port. The dimensions of bolts was determined by the size of the gun, so the heavier the gun, the thicker the bolt.

Above: A close up of the deck planking and the caulking between the planks. Caulking made the seams watertight and consisted of unravelled rope called oakum hammered into the seam followed by hot pitch poured in to complete the joint. Picking oakum, as the process of unravelling was called, and then selling it, is the origin of the saying 'money for old rope', although it was by no means as easy as the modern usage implies.

Below: The chimney from the galley on the gun deck below.

Below: A timberhead fashioned for belaying ropes, with its sharp corners removed to better lead and secure the rope.

Above and left: The ship's bell. Most ships had a ship's bell, and indeed still do. Not only was it used to sound the hours, but it was also used as a signal during fog. As was normal on a warship the bell is housed in a belfry, in *Trincomalee* at the aft end of the fo'c'sle. This bell retains the name of the *Foudroyant*, Wheatley Cobb's first training ship, which had been Nelson's flagship in the Mediterranean in 1799–1800. Bound for the breaker's yard she was bought by Cobb only to then be wrecked in 1897. *Trincomalee* became Cobb's next *Foudroyant* and the bell was transferred to her.

Below: A pin rail at the ship's side complete with belaying pins, while below is a cleat, another fitting for securing ropes. The belaying pins and the cleat could be for sheets or braces in this position. The timberhead to the left is holding the catted anchor stock.

THE UPPER DECK ARMAMENT

The upper deck armament is here made up of a combination of 18-pounder cannon with their distinctive long barrels, and 32-pounder, short-barrelled carronades which were designed for short-range firing. By the end of the Napoleonic Wars the practice was to have only carronades on the upper deck, along with 9-pounder chase guns.

Right: At the fore end of a warship can be found the bow chasers, guns arranged to fire directly ahead. It was usual to have more ports than guns to allow for the gun to be used as part of the broadside as well, and this view shows one of the 18-pounder long cannon on its carriage, at one of the broadside ports on the fo'c'sle deck. Note the heavy breaching tackle securing the gun against its recoil.

Above: The 18-pounder cannon with the two training levers are used to traverse the carriage when aiming to the right or left.

Above: An 18-pounder cannon on its carriage, the design of which had changed little for nearly two hundred years. The quoin, between the training levers, was the basic instrument for elevating the cannon.

Above: The familiar broad arrow mark of a British gun. The mark dates back to Henry VIII's Board of Ordnance in 1544 and was used on a wide range of government issue items.

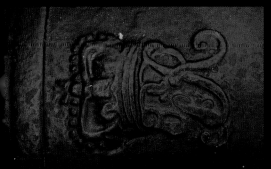

Above: The Georgian royal cipher which was another regular feature of English cast guns.

Above: Elevating guidelines for the cannon. It was a relatively crude guide, but sufficient for the needs of the time when close combat was the order of the day.

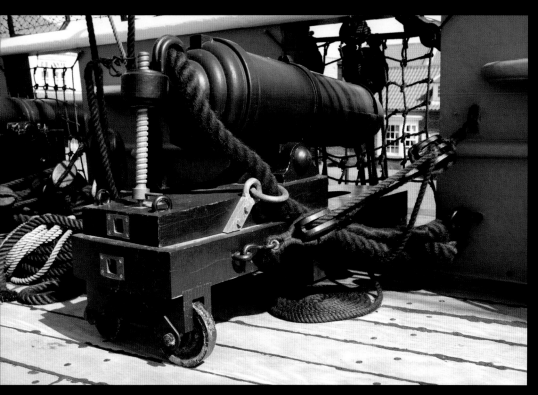

The carronade was named for the Carron Foundry of Falkirk who made and marketed the gun. Popularly ascribed to a minister of the church, in reality it was the end product of experimentation going back several years to a General Melville in 1759. Originally intended as a weapon to defend merchant ships against privateers, its short range meant that in naval use it was best suited to the laying of ships alongside those of an enemy, for anti-personnel fire and to disable rigging, and because of the weight of shot it could fire it could wreak devastating damage at short range. As naval engagements progressed to longer range affairs the carronade ceased to be as effective and after the end of the Napoleonic wars they were gradually abandoned, disappearing completely by the 1830s.

Above and right: A carronade on its mounting. Whilst the carronade was considerably lighter than a cannon, the mounting is clearly more sophisticated than the basic gun carriage. It pivots about a bolt attaching the end of the carriage to the gun port cill – the fighting bolt – and is easily trained on the two wheels, or trucks, fixed fore and aft. The actual carriage sits on top of a slide and the gun is elevated by means of a screw through a screw box at the rear end of the barrel. The rope tackles remain familiar and differ only in placement to those of a carriage gun.

Left: The quarter deck guns, with a 32-pounder carronade in the foreground. The view illustrates well the carronade's traversing carriage compared with the traversing bars for cannon beyond. Note also the difference in size of the displayed shot next to the guns.

Above: The view from the main mast top down to the fo'c'sle along the main fore stays. The name fo'c'sle is an abbreviation of the words fore and castle and dates back to mediaeval times. In the immediate foreground are the two white canvas covered companionways separated by the belfry. Forward of this is the chimney of the galley stove. The two gun ports either side of the lower fore mast are for chase guns, used when pursuing a ship dead ahead.

Right and below: The hammock netting, showing the top ropes and the cranes, the iron uprights along the length of the nets. Once the hammocks were stowed they provided some protection from enemy fire.

Left: One of the two seats of easement intended for use by the crew, showing its somewhat exposed position on the starboard side of the bow.

Main photo: The forward end of the fo'c'sle deck showing clearly the attachments of the main mast fore stay and preventer stay, the bowsprit passing through the bulwark and two ports for the bow chaser guns. At the top of the bulwark are the hammock nets where the crew's hammocks were stowed during the day. Visible through the starboard chase port is the starboard seat of easement. Note the ring bolts for the cannon tackle around the chase ports.

Right: The quick release gear for the anchor. Once the anchor had been cast off from the lashings binding it to the cathead and the ships side, this rope would be the last one holding it to the ship and the hook was arranged to drop the anchor with minimum human intervention.

Below right and bottom: Looking forward from the base of the foremast. The hammock netting stopped short port and starboard to allow access to the bowsprit and the heads.

THE
GUN DECK

The main armament of a frigate was carried on the gun deck. The weather deck above protected this main battery from any falling spars and rigging brought down by enemy fire.

Trincomalee's magnificent replica main armament. As designed she was fitted with 18-pounder cannon shown here in replica, the nearest five being run out for action. That to the right is rigged for sea with the barrel inboard so that its gun port can be closed to prevent ingress of water.

The gun deck of a frigate houses the main armament, the broadside guns. As restored, *Trincomalee* has been fitted out as designed with 18-pounder smooth bore, muzzle-loading cannon. However, during her two commissions she was armed quite differently, although still on the broadside principle. During her first commission the gun deck 18-pounders were replaced by a lesser number of heavier 32-pounders, similar to those to be found on HMS *Victory*'s lower deck, which actually gave her a greater overall weight of shot. For the second commission these were in turn partially replaced by 8-inch shell guns, plus a single 10-inch on the weather deck on a trainable mounting. Subsequently, during her time as a training ship for the Royal Naval Reserve, she would have been fitted with a variety of more modern guns to ensure the reserve sailors were up-to-date in their weapon handling skills.

The after end of the gun deck – looking aft towards the captain's cabin. Although the guns have been run out and the deck is shown otherwise cleared for action, the cabin remains intact. During an action the cabin bulkhead and its contents would also have been cleared away. To the right is the capstan and behind can be seen the brass pillars around the companionway (see inset detail left) that could be folded up and out of the way of the capstan bars when they were in place. Note the main capstan to the right. The drum above the capstan head connects with the capstan head on the deck above. The capstan slots might have had drawers containing bandages, fitted when the ship went into action.

Various rammers and a screw cannon ball extractor can be seen stowed under the deckhead where the training levers were also normally to be found, although alternatively they may have been stowed on the carriage

Far left: One of the beautifully carved barley sugar twist pillars, or stanchions, that were a Wadia trademark of the Bombay Dockyard.

THE 18-POUNDER ARMAMENT

The smooth bore, muzzle-loading cannon was the main weapon of sailing navies from at least Tudor times until the era of the Crimean War in the middle of the nineteenth century, when rifled guns became standard. Breech loading took a little while longer to perfect. Available in a variety of sizes, the Royal Navy introduced standardisation from an early date and by the time *Trincomalee* was built the 18-pounder was the gun specified for this size of frigate. This gun, cast to the pattern developed by Thomas Blomefield who became Inspector of Artillery in 1780, was eight feet long and weighed about 2.5 tons with its carriage. The weapon was also to be found on the upper decks of ships of the line.

Below: This 18-pounder is displayed as rigged for sea with the muzzle lashed to eyebolts above the gun port. The Royal Navy was possibly unique in lashing its guns in this fashion. The French at least at one time favoured loaded guns, ready run out with half gun port lids fitted above and below the barrel, and this arrangement allowed quite a bit more light into the gun deck once the lids had been opened.

Above: A close up of the out-haul tackle on one side of the carriage, used by the gun crew to run out the gun. The recoil would then serve to run the gun back in for reloading.

Above right: From left to right are shown a wad to be placed between the shot and the powder charge; the powder charge itself; and a variety of grape shot, known as case shot. This contained a larger number of smaller balls than the grape shot seen in the picture below.

Right: Various specialist forms of projectile: chain shot and bar shot for destroying an opponent's rigging, and grape shot, a package of nine smaller balls designed to break open and cause as much damage as possible to personnel and fittings.

Right and below right: The tools of the gunner's trade. Here are shown the rammers and the screw extractor (or wad hook) stowed under the deck head. The screw extractor, as its name suggests was used to remove the charge from an already loaded gun. This could be required after a misfire, but more usually after a loaded gun had been kept ready for some time and might need the charge refreshing.

Below: The 18-pounder ready to be run out by the gun crew. Compare this view with that opposite, showing the gun as rigged for sea.

The gun deck, port side, looking towards the bow and the animal manger. The two 18-pounders in the shot are run out, ready for action. Note the gunpowder charge displayed on each carriage, not the place where they would normally be found of course. On the deck in the foreground, lying by the water bucket, is a flexible rope rammer.

Above: The iron riding bitts, introduced to take chain cable. Iron chain imposed a great deal of wear on timber riding bitts and this problem was overcome by various modifications that eventually evolved into the iron riding bitts that can be seen today on *Trincomalee*. The horizontal arms, or barracudas as they were termed, kept the chain links off the wooden decks.

Below left and right: Chain cable replaced hemp cable in the early nineteenth century and patent cable stoppers were developed to hold and control the cable. They were situated in the manger, just aft and in line with the hawse pipes.

Below: The gun deck viewed forward from the starboard side. The wattle fencing held the animals, kept for milk, eggs and meat, within the confines of the manger.

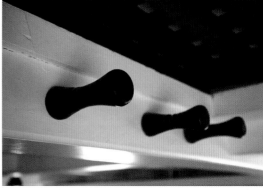

Top left: The sign on the gun deck, exhorting young sailors to 'Remember Nelson', was once mounted above the wheel at the fore end of the built-up after cabin on *Foudroyant*.

Above: Belaying pins positioned in a deck beam adjacent to the grating over the waist which could be used to lash down spars or any other gear stored in the waist.

Left: A row of fire buckets at the ship's centreline. These would have been filled with water prior to going into action. Fire was a major hazard on any wooden ship, but a warship under fire from an enemy was particularly vulnerable.

Below: The 18-pounders on the port side with their training levers. One gun is run in and rigged for sea.

Above: This photograph shows where the main mast passes through the gun deck. At the top can be seen the main mast partners which were made by fitting carlings – short fore-and-aft timbers – of increased scantling, and wedges and baulks of timber that supported the mast where it passed through the deck. Also visible are the topmast and jeer bitts positioned around the mast. In the foreground is an iron cable scuttle, just to the left of the fire buckets,

Right and below: This lever, which appears to have been bent when under strain, is located just under the deckhead. It is not certain what it was for but when lowered (top image) it is in the way of the capstan arm and so may have simply been a brake for the capstan and at some stage bent under enormous pressure.

THE GALLEY

The galley of a frigate of this period was merely a part of the gun deck. This small area contained the Brodie stove, on a tiled section of flooring, and provided the food for the complement of 320 men.

The food was issued to each mess, whose nominated 'Cook' obtained the food from the issuing room on the Orlop deck, prepared it suitably and then handed it into the galley for the actual cooking. The mess cook would then collect it and distribute it

to his mess mates in a fair and equitable fashion. Understandably known as broadside messing, this system lasted in various forms until finally replaced by cafeteria messing after the Second World War.

Various forms of galley stove were used over time, but the most important was probably the Brodie stove that set new standards and, as modified by Lamb and Nicholson in 1811, lasted through to the middle of the nineteenth century

Below: The port side of the Lamb and Nicholson modification of the Brodie stove. Originally designed and patented by one Alexander Brodie, to quote from his patent application, number 1271 of 1780, 'of Carey Street, Chancery Lane, in the County of Middlesex', actually a

Midlands Iron Founder by trade. At the forward end is an open hearth with a built-in turnspit run from an exhaust driven fan for roasting joints of meat. Lamb and Nicholson's modifications produced a similar piece of equipment, but one that was more economical to run.

Above: The starboard side of the Brodie stove which contained, as well as the grate for roasting, two coppers for boiling food, two ovens and separate hanging stoves in which meals could be prepared for officers. The stove was put out in rough weather or during action to prevent sparks setting fire to the surrounding deck, the firehearth extending only a short way from the stove.

Right: Utensils not hung from the iron bars around the stove itself could be stored hanging from bars fitted under the deckhead.

The captain's cabin offered a very spacious accommodation allocation when compared with the rest of the crew. The hierarchy of accommodation space reflected the social distinctions of officers and crew and continues to this day, albeit not so marked as at this time. The captain's cabin served as his office, sleeping quarters, as the command centre for operational planning as well as a place to entertain guests.

In addition to the captain's furniture there are plenty of reminders that this space is part of a working ship. Amongst the other details shown in this view are the four sets of tackles overhead, ready to raise the gun port lids, and the mizzen mast with the bitts either side. In the starboard corner is the captain's hanging cot, opposite his desk on the port side.

As originally designed these four ports would have each had an 18-pounder gun in place, making the cabin rather less spacious than it appears here. As commissioned however *Trincomalee*'s main broadside guns were reduced to 18 32-pounders and these ports would not have been used.

Above: The captain's cabin, looking aft and to port is the best lit part of the ship. Clearly visible are the heavy stern timbers rising up to the weather deck above which keep out little of the light streaming through into the cabin. The doorway leads to the starboard quarter gallery and the latrine, and in this picture the gun port is ajar.

Right: The Marine sentry posted outside the cabin. Not just for security, he was also the captain's receptionist.

Top right: The ropes from the steering wheel above, passing through on their way to the tiller below.

Centre right: The powerful eyebolts were for securing the guns when the cabin was cleared for action and the stern chasers brought in.

Above: Looking forward through to the gun deck, with the captain at his desk. The gun deck is partly lit by a shaft of daylight from the open waist. Note also the two mooring bitts either side of the mizzen mast. In the event of the ship going into action, the bulkhead dividing the cabin from the main run of the deck, would be dismantled.

Left: Navigational instruments: a parallel ruler, telescope and sextant.

Below left: The captain's cot. This is simply a box hung by ropes from hooks in the deckhead and in this case with curtains for a measure of privacy. It might also act as his coffin if the circumstances so required.

Above: The starboard side of the cabin, with a dresser and sideboard. The gun port lid between them has been partially opened using the tackle above.

Right: Detail of the inboard end of the tackle and the chain used to open the gun port lids.

Below: Two external views of the partially opened gun port lid.

Below left: The captain's and officers' seat of ease in the quarter gallery at the stern.

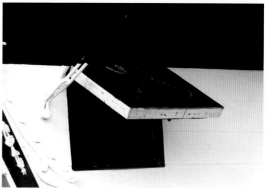

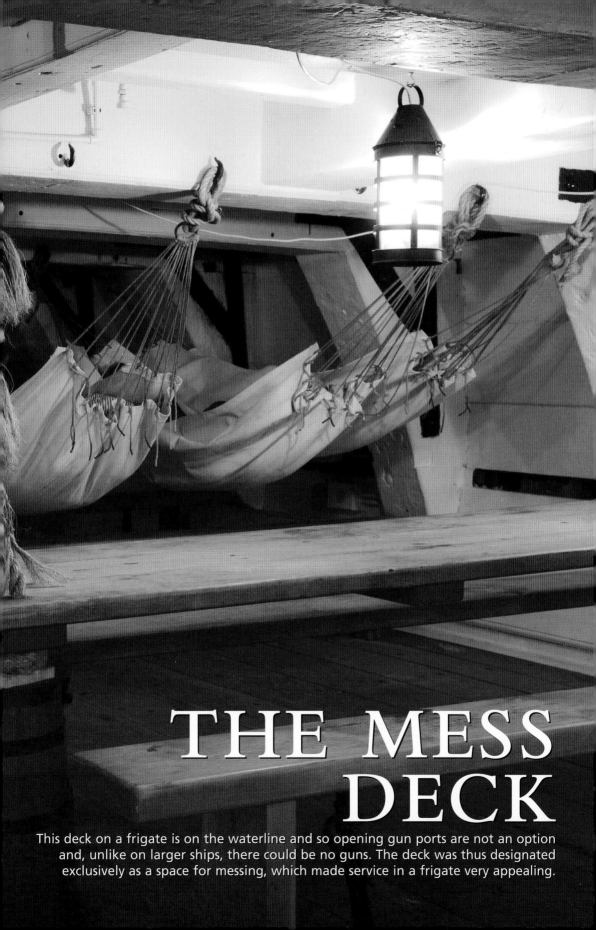

THE MESS DECK

This deck on a frigate is on the waterline and so opening gun ports are not an option and, unlike on larger ships, there could be no guns. The deck was thus designated exclusively as a space for messing, which made service in a frigate very appealing.

ALTHOUGH A FRIGATE'S MESS DECK GAVE
the crew more space for their individual messes the
layout was the same as found on most Royal Navy
ships of the period. Each mess of eight to ten men had
a table and benches, a bread bin under the hanging
end of the table and a bucket of hot water. When the
table was not set for a meal the platters and mugs
would be stowed away in the cupboard at the
outboard side of each mess. Although often given as
the origin of the term 'a square meal' there is little
evidence that the square platters did in fact form the
basis for the expression, which in this context would
seem to simply refer to an honest meal and is
American in origin.

Below: Hammocks were hung above the mess tables between
the beams, and the hammock hooks above the table are
clearly visible. Many sailors claimed that the hammock was the
most comfortable bed they'd ever slept in.

Above: A mess table, hung from the deck beam above, and laid out for a meal. Hammocks have been stored away for the day. The iron plate knees in the background were used to reinforce the hanging knees below each deck beam. As timber became scarcer and suitable pieces for making curved knees could no longer be found, it became necessary to use iron in combination with the timber chocks to fashion a knee. The iron plate was basically triangular in shape with a short length at right angles running along the ship's side.

Right: The main mast passing through the mast partners to the mast step on the keelson below. The open grating behind the mast gives access to the orlop deck below, while in front are hot water buckets.

Left: The Seppings iron tiller located above the bread room aft of the wardroom. The chains visible passing under the deckhead are the modern mooring chains, but otherwise this compartment is much as it would have been in 1817. The large curved timbers sweeping up to the transom timbers are the transom knees, or sleepers. The upright timber is the sternson knee attached to the sternpost on which the rudder is hung. The lines controlling the tiller lead to double sheaves (left of photo, under the tiller) greatly increasing the purchase.

Above: The extreme end of the tiller showing the blocks which carry the hemp ropes from the steering wheel. A completely manually powered system, it would have needed several men on the wheel in bad weather and if it was really bad there would have been a team in this compartment on relieving tackles easing the load for those on the wheel above.

Below left: The aft end of the mess deck with the access to the orlop deck below. Just visible beyond the bulkhead is the officers' wardroom.

Above: An iron hanging knee. These would become the norm after Sepping's refinements and may be a later addition to the vessel.

Right: Unlike on modern ships, the anchor cable of a Napoleonic era warship was stowed amidships. The cable was hauled in by attaching it to a closed loop of cable, known as the messenger which was run around the main capstan. The attachment was by a piece of rope known as a nip and the boys who did the work became 'nippers', a name still widely used for young boys.

Below: An iron chain compressor which functioned as a break to prevent the cable running out. This is a later addition when the mooring cables were changed to chain. The movement of the arm was controlled by a single purchase block and tackle.

THE WARDROOM

The officers of a warship messed in the wardroom. The etymology of this word is not particularly clear but would seem to have a common old English root as warden for example, meaning guardian or protector.

Conventionally the wardroom was reserved for commissioned officers; the warrant officers, midshipmen and cadets would have been messed in the gunroom, which in a ship of the line was usually one deck below the wardroom. However, with no room for a gunroom in a frigate it seems that all these ranks shared the wardroom.

Left and below: The wardroom table set for dinner, viewed looking forwards. The officers were served by a steward who prepared their food in a similar fashion to the crews' mess cooks, drawing rations from the issuing room and having it cooked on the galley stove on the gun deck. In addition, the officers would often have arranged an extra supply of provisions to improve their meals.

On either side of the table can be seen the individual officer's cabins, while the skylight above gives the only natural light to the space.

Right: A typical officer's cabin. In this case it is that of the Royal Marine officer, but is typical of these cabins in content and layout. Note the hanging cot, folding chair and small bureau. Ventilation would have been limited to air circulating though the slatted door, and lighting to a single oil lamp or candle.

Below right: A view from outside the wardroom area which gives a good impression of the row of cabins, in this instance those on the port side, looking aft.

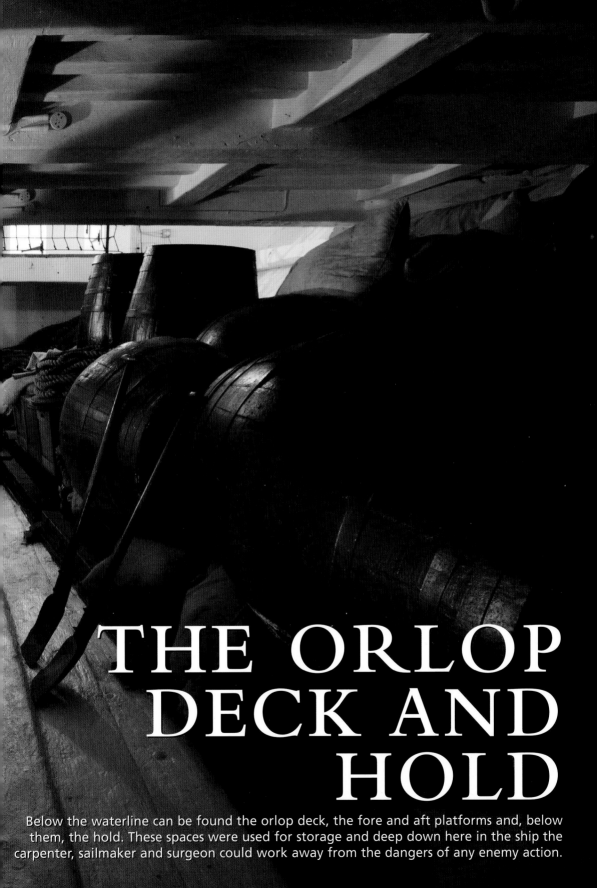

THE ORLOP DECK AND HOLD

Below the waterline can be found the orlop deck, the fore and aft platforms and, below them, the hold. These spaces were used for storage and deep down here in the ship the carpenter, sailmaker and surgeon could work away from the dangers of any enemy action.

A general view of the hold and, above, the orlop deck or platform. One of the few criticisms of this class of frigate was that there was insufficient stowage for more than three months at sea. This was as a result of the basic shape of the hull which was quite fine at the ends to help it achieve the speeds for which it was known. In this view we see an incompletely stored ship: the large barrels or casks, for beer and salt meat, would normally rest on a bed of shingle spread over the pig iron ballast (see previous page). Here the ballast has been neatly stowed rather than spread uniformly over the hull bottom, allowing the visitor to see the wooden structure of the latter. The name orlop is usually used for the deck above the cask stowage, whilst the ends are known as platforms. Here on the orlop can be seen the sail room with a sailmaker at work. Also on this platform would be the carpenter's and boatswain's stores.

Left: An iron hanging knee very similar to the ones used on the deck above *(see page 115)*. Clearly visible is the iron wedge within the triangle, that was driven in between the chock, or knee, and the beam above. When the ship worked in a sea, or if the timbers shrank, the wedge could be driven further in to tighten the whole structure.

Above: The port side of the hold showing the lodging knees and beams of the orlop deck. The lodging knees are ingeniously fashioned, straight and curved, to fit in the narrow space between the beams. The carlings, running fore and aft, are neatly fitted between the beams and the knees.

Below: The breadroom beneath the aft platform. Note the use of iron here as breasthooks or crutches. In the rack to the left, in this cool part of the ship, are stored cheeses.

Above: Part of the hold with a tackle rigged to aid moving stores around. Note the knee reinforcing the bulkhead attachment to the ship's side, and the steps leading up to the access to the carpenter's walk.

Left: The carpenter at work, stiffening up some caulking from the carpenter's walk. It was this space that allowed access to the side of the ship beneath the waterline to inspect and repair any damage to the hull.

Below: The mast step, which was a massive baulk of timber, usually oak, set over the keelson, into which the foot of a mast was fitted, but not fixed, employing a mortice and tenon joint. The modern masts displayed here, however, are hollow steel which encourages ventilation in this part of the ship.

Above: A view looking along the carpenter's walk. This was a very cramped space, only 4ft 4in high, but just big enough to allow access to the carpenter and his crew so that they could inspect and, where necessary, repair the hull of the ship from the inside. The deck is formed of gratings that allowed ventilation of the hold and the penetration of a little light. To the left of the picture is the sail room, on the orlop, or midships platform.

Right: A view into the magazine. The clear bulkhead is a modern addition to allow the visitor to see into the magazine. No naked flames were allowed anywhere near the gunpowder, so the gunners mates would have worked by the light of a lantern behind a glass window in the lamp room alongside the magazine.

Above: The ship's doctor in his store on the aft platform. Essentially a surgeon, the doctor was also required to treat the many injuries sustained by the crew when working the ship as well as the illnesses such as scurvy that at one time plagued the long distance sailor.

Right: The gunner's store, or armory, was used for storage of small arms as well as the tools of his trade. Here is shown a box of 'Brown Bess' muskets, more properly known as the Sea Service Musket. Somewhat shorter than the army musket, the Sea Service musket was in use from 1778 to 1854.

Bottom right: Part of the boatswain's store, just aft of the forward platform. with spare rope and tackles ready for use where required.

SOURCES

BIBLIOGRAPHY

Brown, DK *Before the Ironclad, Development of Ship Design, Propulsion and Armament in the Royal Navy, 1815–60*, (Conway, 1990).

Coad, Jonathan *Support for the Fleet: architecture and engineering of the Royal Navy's bases 1700-1914* (English Heritage, 2014)

Colgate, H A 'The Royal Navy and Trincomalee',*Ceylon Journal of Historical and Social Studies*, 1964, Vol 7 No 1.

Crimmin, P K 'The Supply of Timber for the Royal Navy c1803 to c1830', in *The Naval Miscellany,* Volume 7, Susan Rose, (Navy Records Society Publications, July 2008).

Ferreiro, Larrie D *Ships and Science, The Birth of Naval Architecture in the Scientific Revolution, 1600–1800*, (MIT Press, 2010).

Gardiner, Robert *The Heavy Frigate, Eighteen Pounder Frigates*, (Conway, 1994).

——, *The Sailing Frigate, A History in Ship Models*, (Seaforth, 2012).

Goodwin, Peter *The Construction and Fitting of the Sailing Man of War, 1650–1850*, (Conway, 2001 reprint).

Kemp, P (ed.) *The Oxford Companion to Ships and the Sea* (Oxford University Press, 1976)

Lambert, Andrew *Trincomalee, the Last of Nelson's Frigates*, (Chatham Publishing, 2002).

Lavery, Brian *Nelson's Navy, The Ships, Men and Organisation, 1793–1815*, (Conway, 2000 reprint).

——, *The Arming and Fitting of English Ships of War 1600-1815* (Conway, 1987)

Lyon, David & Winfield, Rif *The Sail and Steam Navy List: All the Ships of the Royal Navy 1815-1889* (Chatham Publishing, 2004)

Peterson, Lennarth, *Rigging Period Ship Models* (Seaforth Publishing, 2011)

Pulvertaft, David *Figureheads of the Royal Navy* (Seaforth Publishing, 2012)

Schlich, W *Schlich's Manual of Forestry*, 3rd Edition, (Bradbury, Agnew and Co. Ltd. 1906).

Toll, Ian W *Six Frigates, How Piracy, War and British Supremacy at Sea gave Birth to the World's Most Powerful Navy*, (Michael Joseph, 2006).

Walker, Fred M, *Ships & Shipbuilders: Pioneers of Design and Construction* (Seaforth Publishing, 2010)

From Trincomalee to Portsea, The Diary of Eliza Bunt 1818–1822, Transcribed and explained by Mary Hope Monnery. Kindle edition, The Friends of HMS *Trincomalee*. 20 Dec 2012.

WEBSITES

http://www.newforest.hampshire.org.uk/

http://www.sainiksamachar.nic.in/englisharchives/2010/dec01-10/h5.htm

http://en.wikisource.org/wiki/Page:A_Naval_Biographical_Dictionary.djvu/137

ACKNOWLEDGEMENTS

The authors and publisher would like to thank the staff and volunteers of HMS *Trincomalee* who contributed so much to the production of this book, particularly David McKnight, Chief Executive and General Manager, and also David Lilley, Bob Monsen and Ryan Auton who maintain the vessel so beautifully and have a remarkable store of knowledge which they generously shared; Colin Baxter for the use of his watercolour of *Trincomalee* arriving in Portsmouth, and his memories of *Foudroyant*; Suzanne Heywood at Teesside University for helping to track down illustrations; and Matthew Sheldon at the National Museum of the Royal Navy for help on the Royal Navy's use of the port of *Trincomalee*.